83

CliffsNotes™

D1192603

Homer's
Iliad

By Bob Linn

IN THIS BOOK

- Learn about the Life and Background of the Author

- Preview an Introduction to the Epic Poem

- Explore themes, character development, and recurring images in the Critical Commentaries

- Examine in-depth Character Analyses

- Acquire an understanding of the novel with Critical Essays

- Reinforce what you learn with CliffsNotes Review

- Find additional information in CliffsNotes Resource Center and online at www.cliffsnotes.com

IDG Books Worldwide, Inc.
An International Data Group Company
Foster City, CA • Chicago, IL • Indianapolis, IN • New York, NY

About the Author

Bob Linn is a high school teacher in Georgia and has a Ph.D.

Publisher's Acknowledgments

Editorial

Project Editor: Sherri Fugit
Acquisitions Editor: Greg Tubach
Copy Editor: Rowena Rappaport
Glossary Editors: The editors and staff of Webster's New World Dictionaries
Editorial Administrator: Michelle Hacker

Production

Proofreader: York Production Services, Inc.
Indexer: York Production Services, Inc.
IDG Books Indianapolis Production Department

CliffsNotes™ Homer's *Iliad*
Published by
IDG Books Worldwide, Inc.
An International Data Group Company
919 E. Hillsdale Blvd.
Suite 400
Foster City, CA 94404

www.idgbooks.com (IDG Books Worldwide Web site)

www.cliffsnotes.com (CliffsNotes Web site)

Copyright © 2000 IDG Books Worldwide, Inc. All rights reserved. No part of this book, including interior design, cover design, and icons, may be reproduced or transmitted in any form, by any means (electronic, photocopying, recording, or otherwise) without the prior written permission of the publisher.

ISBN: 0-7645-8586-X

Printed in the United States of America

10 9 8 7 6 5 4 3 2 1

1O/TQ/QV/QQ/IN

Distributed in the United States by IDG Books Worldwide, Inc.

Library of Congress Cataloging-in-Publication Data

Linn, Bob.
    CliffNotes Homer's Iliad / by Bob Linn.
        p.   cm.
    Includes index.
    ISBN 0-7645-8586-X (alk. paper)
    1. Homer. Iliad--Examinations--Study guides.
2. Epic Poetry, Greek--Examinations--Study guides.
3. Achilles (Greek mythology) in literature. 4. Trojan War in literature. I. Title: Homer's Iliad. II Title.
PA4037.Z5 L56 2000
883'.0--dc11   00-038848
                                                      CIP

Distributed by CDG Books Canada Inc. for Canada; by Transworld Publishers Limited in the United Kingdom; by IDG Norge Books for Norway; by IDG Sweden Books for Sweden; by IDG Books Australia Publishing Corporation Pty. Ltd. for Australia and New Zealand; by TransQuest Publishers Pte Ltd. for Singapore, Malaysia, Thailand, Indonesia, and Hong Kong; by Gotop Information Inc. for Taiwan; by ICG Muse, Inc. for Japan; by Intersoft for South Africa; by Eyrolles for France; by International Thomson Publishing for Germany, Austria and Switzerland; by Distribuidora Cuspide for Argentina; by LR International for Brazil; by Galileo Libros for Chile; by Ediciones ZETA S.C.R. Ltda. for Peru; by WS Computer Publishing Corporation, Inc., for the Philippines; by Contemporanea de Ediciones for Venezuela; by Express Computer Distributors for the Caribbean and West Indies; by Micronesia Media Distributor, Inc. for Micronesia; by Chips Computadoras S.A. de C.V. for Mexico; by Editorial Norma de Panama S.A. for Panama; by American Bookshops for Finland.

For general information on IDG Books Worldwide's books in the U.S., please call our Consumer Customer Service department at **800-762-2974**. For reseller information, including discounts and premium sales, please call our Reseller Customer Service department at **800-434-3422**.

For information on where to purchase IDG Books Worldwide's books outside the U.S., please contact our International Sales department at **317-596-5530 or fax 317-572-4002.**

For consumer information on foreign language translations, please contact our Customer Service department at **1-800-434-3422**, fax 317-572-4002, or e-mail rights@idgbooks.com.

For information on licensing foreign or domestic rights, please phone **+1-650-653-7098.**

For sales inquiries and special prices for bulk quantities, please contact our Order Services department at **800-434-3422** or write to the address above.

For information on using IDG Books Worldwide's books in the classroom or for ordering examination copies, please contact our Educational Sales department at **800-434-2086** or fax **317-572-4005.**

For press review copies, author interviews, or other publicity information, please contact our Public Relations department at **650-653-7000** or fax **650-653-7500.**

For authorization to photocopy items for corporate, personal, or educational use, please contact Copyright Clearance Center, 222 Rosewood Drive, Danvers, MA 01923, or fax **978-750-4470.**

Table of Contents

How to Use This Book

CliffsNotes Homer's *Iliad* supplements the original work, giving you background information about Homer, an introduction to the poem, a graphical character map, critical commentaries, expanded glossaries, and a comprehensive index. CliffsNotes Review tests your comprehension of the original text and reinforces learning with questions and answers, practice projects, and more. For further information on Homer and the *Iliad,* check out the CliffsNotes Resource Center.

CliffsNotes provides the following icons to highlight essential elements of particular interest:

Reveals the underlying themes in the work.

Helps you to more easily relate to or discover the depth of a character.

Uncovers elements such as setting, atmosphere, mystery, passion, violence, irony, symbolism, tragedy, foreshadowing, and satire.

Enables you to appreciate the nuances of words and phrases.

Don't Miss Our Web Site

Discover classic literature as well as modern-day treasures by visiting the CliffsNotes Web site at www.cliffsnotes.com. You can obtain a quick download of a CliffsNotes title, purchase a title in print form, browse our catalog, or view online samples.

You'll also find interactive tools that are fun and informative, links to interesting Web sites, tips, articles, and additional resources to help you, not only for literature, but for test prep, finance, careers, computers, and the Internet too. See you at www.cliffsnotes.com!

LIFE AND BACKGROUND OF THE POET

Life and Background of the Poet

Little can be said about Homer. Ancient Greek tradition, as well as a study of the language and style of the poems, indicates that he probably lived and wrote sometime in the eighth or ninth centuries B.C., but no more definite date can be determined. In ancient times, seven different cities claimed the honor of having been his birthplace. None of these assertions can be validated. However, Homer may have come from the island of Chios, on the western coast of Asia Minor—in earlier times, a family of the same name lived there and claimed him as an ancestor, and devoted themselves to the recitation of his works. Whether he came from Chios or not, it is highly probable that Homer was a native and resident of some part of Eastern Greece or Asia Minor, for the dialect he used in his works is that of the Asian Greeks.

Tradition has it that Homer was blind, but the evidence for this idea is unreliable. This evidence is based on the portrayal in the *Odyssey* of a blind minstrel who sings a poem about the fall of Troy. But there is no reason to believe that the poet was describing himself in this scene. Throughout the two epics, no consistent autobiographical information exists, and no other literature of the period survives that describes the poet.

The early Greeks insisted that there was a single individual named Homer, to whom they ascribed the *Iliad*, the *Odyssey*, and several minor works called the *Homeric Hymns*. However, around the third century B.C., the so-called Homeric Question was first propounded. Several of the grammarians of the time asserted that the *Iliad* and the *Odyssey* were actually composed by two different writers. At various times, later European critics supported this view. Another school of thought, especially popular in the nineteenth century, claims that Homer never lived, and that the two epics are the collective works of groups of anonymous bards to whom the name Homer was later applied. These scholars suggest that the two poems were constantly revised and added to whenever they were recited and did not reach their present form until the 6th century B.C. when, in Athens, they were written down for the first time.

Whatever one thinks of the existence of Homer, certain facts concerning the composition of the *Iliad* are firmly established. Originally, it was an oral composition meant to be sung or chanted for an audience. Research, particularly on living bards in the former Yugoslavia, has shown that epic length poems are composed and presented through a combination of stock phrases and scenes coupled with extemporaneous composition. The *Iliad* shows evidence of similar elements. Stock phrases and scenes exist in the epithets for character ("old Gerenian Nestor"), descriptions of natural settings such as dawn, battle preparation scenes, and the battle scenes themselves. Set speeches may also be used. Agamemnon's speech s echoed in a speech by Odysseus in the *Odyssey*. The catalogue of ships in Book II is also such a set piece, although it was probably added after the poem was written.

Generally, contemporary scholarship believes that the *Iliad* and the *Odyssey* have a consistency of style and outlook indicating that they are the work of one writer. That a man named Homer actually composed the *Iliad* and the *Odyssey* as an original and entirely individual composition as Virgil composed the *Aeneid* seems highly doubtful. Various time references and other irregularities in the poems suggest that parts of the poems were written in entirely different periods of Greek history. However, the obvious structural complexity and thematic unity of the poems as well as their set metrical pattern of dactylic hexameter indicate a single author of great sophistication. As with the great English epic, *Beowulf*, the *Iliad* and the *Odyssey* may have existed as oral tradition for some time and eventually were put into final, written form by a single poetic genius. The poet may have composed the epics himself, or he may have borrowed from the works of earlier bards. Because the people living nearest to the era of the composition of the poems believed them to be the product of one hand, the modern critic accepts this view and attributes the stylistic differences between the two epic poems to their having been composed at different stages in the poet's life and to the different themes of the works. Rather than take a defensive or apologetic position, the contemporary scholar insists that the burden of proof be on those who deny the existence of Homer. To date, this position has not been successfully challenged.

While little if anything is known of Homer's life, his works are an everlasting tribute to him. For thousands of years, the *Iliad* and the *Odyssey* have been the standards by which poets of all languages have measured themselves. Homer is unsurpassed in his understanding of human nature in all its aspects, for his keen observation of the world in which people live, for his essential sanity and good taste, and for his superb control of all the technical devices of his medium.

Background of the Epic

The Greeks, or Achaians, that Homer writes about in the *Iliad* were not people of a unified nation. Instead, areas of the Balkan Peninsula, now known as Greece, were made up of many small kingdoms, populated by ethnically-related peoples, from 1400–800 B.C., and even later, to the time of Alexander the Great (c. 200 B.C.). Scholarship generally dates the composition of the *Iliad* at about 800 B.C. At that time, Homer would have been writing about the Mycenaeans, a people who lived in Greece four to five hundred years earlier, although the picture he paints in the epic shows aspects of society from all of the periods between 1400 and 800 B.C.

The Mycenaeans, also called Hellenes, had taken control of the Balkan Peninsula around 1500 B.C. They formed what were essentially small farming communities organized around a predominant family. In the *Iliad*, each of the great warrior heroes is the head, and therefore the king of each of these communities. According to legend, and evidenced by some archaeological finds, the most powerful of these communities was Mycenae, ruled by Agamemnon. These rulers were known as *basileis*, and they acted as kings, generals, and judges. The noble families in each kingdom were the *aristoi*, who advised the basileis through a council called the *boule*. Ordinary soldiers were known as the *laos*, but they too had a voice and could vote in the *agora*, or public forum, on decisions that involved them.

In the *Iliad*, the Greek characters act as a kind of state. Agamemnon is the *basileis*; the other individual rulers act as the *aristoi*. The common soldiers, or *laos*, are best typified by Thersites, who speaks up at the *boule*, or assembly, in Book II.

Originally, the Mycenaeans were sea raiders. Their power and progress came as a result of conquest, usually carried out by groups organized from several kingdoms. The goal of these raids was to acquire goods, raw materials, and slaves. The slaves were usually women, because the Mycenaean custom was to kill all the men of a conquered state and capture the women and children.

Political decisions within the Mycenaean State were made through assemblies. Typically, these assemblies were made up of the powerful men within a particular state. However, for more far-reaching and important matters involving war and raids, an assembly of the leaders of a group of states would be arranged. Such major decisions were made through discussion and debate.

At the same time the Mycenaeans came to power in Greece, a related kingdom, Troy, developed near the northern coast of Asia Minor (modern-day Turkey). Archaeologists date the original city at the Troy site as early as 3000 B.C. By 1500 B.C., Troy was a flourishing, walled fortress, famed for horses and natural resources such as iron. The people who inhabited Troy were related to the Mycenaean Greeks and possibly traded with them.

Heinrich Schliemann, an amateur archaeologist, using information in the *Iliad* and other Greek texts, discovered the site that is now accepted as Troy at an area called Hisarlik. Schliemann also found Mycenae on the Greek mainland. Schliemann's work and that of others revealed that a number of cities were built on the Troy site, each new one on the ruins of a previous city. Evidence at the city labeled site VIIA revealed that it was destroyed by fire, which was typically the fate of cities conquered by Greek raiders. Further evidence revealed that site VIIA was involved in a siege—remains of bodies there showed signs of sudden, violent death.

These facts about both Mycenae and Troy point toward a reality that may underlie the romanticized story of the *Iliad*. Sometime around 1200 B.C., a Mycenaean raiding party attacked the walled fortress of Troy. This attack may have resulted from a break in the rules of hospitality—a Trojan steals the wife of a Greek—but more likely it was a simple raid for booty and slaves. Troy proves to be no easy conquest; but eventually the city is taken and destroyed with mixed profits and results for the Greeks involved.

This scenario is, of course, pure speculation, but it fits with both the archaeological evidence and the basic story of the *Iliad*. More than this basic scenario would be absolute fiction. Are the names of the heroes in the *Iliad* the real names of Mycenaean and Trojan warriors? Did a Greek warrior refuse to fight? Did the Greek forces breach the walls of Troy with a subterfuge involving horses? No one will ever be able to answer these questions; they exist in a poem and nowhere else. At best, the possibility exists that parts of the story of the *Iliad* are based on fact. Nothing in the historical or archaeological record disproves the idea that a Mycenaean raiding party could have sacked a city in Asia Minor called Troy.

INTRODUCTION TO THE POEM

Introduction to the Poem

The *Iliad* deals with only a small portion of the Trojan War; in fact, it covers only a few months during the tenth year of that war. The ancient Greek audience, however, would have been familiar with all the events leading up to this tenth year, and during the course of the *Iliad*, Homer makes many references to various past events.

The story of the *Iliad* has its actual beginning in the creation of the great wall at Troy. The Trojans enlisted the aid of the sea god, Poseidon, to help build the wall. However, after the wall was constructed, Poseidon demanded his just compensation, but the Trojans reneged. Consequently, Troy was without divine protection and, in fact, Poseidon became its enemy.

At the time of the Trojan war, Troy was ruled by King Priam, who was married to Hekuba. According to legend, Priam and Hekuba had forty-nine children, including the warrior Hektor, the prophetess Cassandra, and the young lover, Paris (also known as Alexandros). Deiphobus is also one of the children of Priam and Hekuba.

When Hekuba was pregnant with Paris, she had a dream that Paris would be the cause of the destruction of Troy. An oracle and a seer confirmed that this son would indeed be the cause of the total destruction of the noble city of Troy. Therefore, for the sake of the city, Hekuba agreed to abandon her newborn infant to die by exposure on Mount Ida, but Paris was saved by shepherds and grew up as a shepherd, ignorant of his royal birth.

The *Iliad* begins: The judgement of Paris

On the Greek side, the story of the *Iliad* begins with the wedding of Peleus, a mortal, and Thetis, a goddess. These two become the parents of Achilles. At their wedding, Eris, the goddess of strife, throws down a golden apple with the message, "For the Fairest." Hera, Athena, and Aphrodite all try to claim the prize, and no god, including Zeus, is willing to resolve the dispute.

After a long conference on Mount Ida, Paris, the poor but royal shepherd is chosen to be the judge of the dispute between the three goddesses. They all offer bribes to Paris. Hera offers him rule over all of Asia. Athena offers victory in battle and supreme wisdom. But Aphrodite, knowing her man, offers the most beautiful woman in the world, Helen, wife of Menelaos, the ruler of Sparta. Paris proclaims Aphrodite the fairest of all and anticipates his prize.

The initiation of strife, in the form of Eris and her apple, at the wedding of Peleus and Thetis, introduces an idea that runs throughout the *Iliad*. Strife, metaphorically embodied in a goddess in the legend, is the motivating factor in most of the major events in the epic. Strife provokes the war. Strife with Agamemnon over a slave girl causes Achilles to withdraw from battle. Strife between various groups and individuals sharpens the action of the poem. Finally, the resolution of strife provides an ending for the poem. Eris is rarely mentioned in the *Iliad*, but her presence is almost palpable.

Before going to the court of Menelaos to secure Helen, Paris establishes his legitimacy as a son of King Priam of Troy. Only then does Paris travel to Sparta, where for ten days he is treated royally as the guest of Menelaos and Helen. After ten days, Menelaos has to travel to Crete to conduct business. In Menelaos' absence, Paris abducts Helen and returns with her to Troy. Various accounts of this event make Helen either a willing accomplice to Paris' scheme or a resisting victim of kidnapping. In the *Iliad*, Helen's constant references to herself as a bitch and prostitute leave little doubt that Homer sees her as a culpable accomplice in the abduction.

Word of Helen's abduction reaches Menelaos in Crete. He immediately goes to his brother, Agamemnon, the great ruler of Mycenae. At first the two brothers try diplomacy with Troy to secure the return of Helen. When that fails, they determine to enlist the aid of many other rulers of small Greek kingdoms. Nestor of Pylos, an old friend of the family, accompanies Menelaos as he goes to each state seeking support. The Greek army that Menelaos and Nestor help assemble represents the Greek or Mycenaean notion of reciprocity. Actions were performed with the expectation of a reciprocal action. According to some accounts, the various Greek rulers had all courted Helen and felt an obligation to Menelaos. But, even so, they go on the raid with an understanding that they will receive a share of the booty that will come from the destruction of Troy and other nearby states. In fact, the opening dispute between Agamemnon and Achilles is over what they each see as inequity in the distribution of their war prizes.

Some of the Greek leaders were anxious to sack Troy; but two, Odysseus and Achilles, were warned by the oracles of their fates if they participated in the war. Odysseus was warned that his journey home would last twenty years, and thus he feigned madness; but his ruse was quickly discovered and he finally agreed to go to war. The Greeks knew that they could never capture Troy without the help of Achilles, who was the greatest warrior in the world. He was practically invulnerable as a fighter, because at birth his mother dipped him in the River Styx, rendering him immortal everywhere except in the heel, where she held him. (Later, Paris discovers this vulnerability and shoots a poisoned arrow into Achilles' heel—thus, we have the term "Achilles' heel," meaning one's vulnerability.) Achilles was warned that if he went to war he would gain great glory, but he would die young. His mother then disguised him in women's clothing, but the sly Odysseus discovered the trick and Achilles finally consented to go.

After a few months, the Greek army gathers at Aulis in Euboea. According to some accounts, they immediately launch an attack on Teuthrania, an ally of Troy, are defeated, and are driven back. Much of the army disperses. During this same period, the prophet Kalchas predicts that ten years will pass before the walls of Troy will fall. The Greeks, or Achaians as they called themselves, do not try a mass attack on Troy again for about eight years. They have not, as many imagine, spent nine years beneath the walls of Troy, as when the *Iliad* opens. Some scholars consider this first expedition story to be a variant account of the more common story, but many others think that the expedition against Troy was actually made up of two widely separated expeditions.

The story of the second (or possibly first) assembly at Aulis is the more famous account. At this assembly of the Achaian forces, they are unable to sail because of onshore winds. This time Kalchas reports that Artemis, Goddess of the Hunt, is offended because Agamemnon killed a deer sacred to her. The only way the Achaians can leave is by Agamemnon's sacrifice of his daughter, Iphigeneia, to Artemis. Agamemnon tricks Iphigeneia by telling her that she is to wed Achilles. When she arrives for her wedding, she is gagged so that she cannot pronounce a dying curse, and sacrificed to Artemis. The winds shift, and the Achaians (Greeks) sail for Troy.

The Achaians land at a protected shore near Troy. They build a wall of earth, stone, and timber to protect their ships. This wall is the focus of the Trojan attack in Books XII and XIII. After the construction of the wall, the Achaians begin their siege of Troy. Some of their forces raid nearby states. Achilles attacks cities to the south while Telamonian Aias (Ajax) takes Teuthrania.

A year later, the tenth year since the original prediction by Kalchas, all of the Achaians assemble near Troy to begin what they hope will be the final assault. Here is where the *Iliad* begins as a feud develops between Achilles and Agamemnon. The poem recounts the events of this feud as they take place over several days. The epic ends with the death and burial of the Trojan warrior, Hektor.

After the *Iliad*: The fall of Troy

The events after the *Iliad* that lead to the fall of Troy are not a part of the poem. After the burial of Hektor, the Trojans call on outside forces for help, and the Greeks lose many warriors. In one battle, Achilles encounters Paris, who shoots an arrow that, guided by Apollo, strikes Achilles in the right heel, the only place where he is vulnerable. Aias (Ajax) and Odysseus are able, with great difficulty, to rescue Achilles' body, and immediately there arises a dispute over who should receive Achilles' splendid armor. When it is awarded to Odysseus, Aias (Ajax) becomes so furious that he threatens to kill some of the Greek leaders. When he realizes the lack of honor in his threats, he commits suicide.

With the death of their two greatest and most valiant warriors, Aias and Achilles, the Greeks become anxious about ever taking Troy. After consulting various seers and oracles, they are instructed to secure the bow and arrows of Heracles, which are in the hands of Prince Philoctetes, a Greek who was abandoned earlier because of a loathsome wound that would not heal. Odysseus and Diomedes are sent to Philoctetes, and they convince him to return with the bow and arrows. In his first encounter in battle, he is able to kill Paris. This death, however, does not affect the course of the war.

The Greeks are then given a series of tasks that they must accomplish to secure victory: They must bring the bones of Pelops back to Greece from Asia, bring Achilles' son into the war, and steal the sacred image of Athena from the Trojan sanctuary. These tasks are accomplished, but none of them changes the course of the war. Then Odysseus conceives a plan whereby the Greeks can get inside the walls of Troy: A great horse of wood is constructed with a hollow belly that can hold many warriors. In the darkness of night, the horse is brought to the Trojan plain. Odysseus and some of his men are hidden inside the horse. The rest of the Achaians burn their camps and sail off behind a nearby island.

The next morning, the Trojans find the Greeks gone and the huge, mysterious horse sitting before Troy. They also discover a Greek named Sinon, whom they take captive. Odysseus provided Sinon with plausible stories about the Greek departure, the wooden horse, and his own presence there to tell the Trojans. Sinon tells Priam and the others that Athena deserted the Greeks because of the theft of her image from her temple. Without her help, they were lost and so they departed. But to get home safely, they had to have a human sacrifice. Sinon was chosen, but he escaped and hid. The horse was left to placate the angry goddess, and the Greeks hoped the Trojans would desecrate it, earning Athena's hatred. These lies convince Priam and many other Trojans, so they pull the gigantic horse inside the gates to honor Athena.

That night, the soldiers creep out of the horse, kill the sentries, and open the gates to let the Achaian army in. The Achaians set fires throughout the city, massacre the inhabitants, and loot the city. The Trojan resistance is ineffectual. King Priam is killed, and by morning all but a few Trojans are dead. Only Aeneas, with his old father, his young son, and a small band of Trojans, escape. Hektor's young son, Astyanax, is thrown from the walls of the city. The women who are left are given to the Greek leaders as war prizes, to be used as slaves or as concubines. Troy is devastated. Hera and Athena have their revenge upon Paris and upon his city.

Brief Synopsis

The Achaians, under King Agamemnon, have been fighting the Trojans off and on for nine years, trying to retrieve Helen, the wife of Menelaos, and thus Agamemnon's sister-in-law. Paris, a son of the king of Troy, kidnaps Helen, who becomes the legendary "Helen of Troy" and "the woman with the face that launched a thousand ships."

Yet, after years of Achaian attacks, Troy remains intact, and the Trojan army remains undefeated. The same cannot be said for the Achaian army. At present, the Achaian troops are dying from a mysterious plague. Hundreds of funeral pyres burn nightly. Finally, Achilles, the Achaians' most honored soldier, calls for an assembly to determine the cause of the plague.

A soothsayer reveals to the army that King Agamemnon's arrogance caused the deadly plague; he refused to return a woman who was captured and awarded to him as a "war prize." Reluctantly, Agamemnon agrees to return the woman, but, as compensation, he says that he will take the woman who was awarded to Achilles, his best warrior.

Achilles is furious, and he refuses to fight any longer for the Achaians. He and his forces retreat to the beach beside their ships, and Achilles asks his mother, the goddess Thetis, if she will ask Zeus, king of the gods, to help the Trojans defeat his former comrades, the Achaians. Zeus agrees to do so.

The two armies prepare for battle, and Paris (the warrior who kidnapped Menelaos' wife, Helen) leaps out and challenges any of the Achaians to a duel. Menelaos challenges him and beats him, but before Paris is killed, the goddess Aphrodite whisks him away to the safety of his bedroom in Troy.

A short truce is called, but it is broken when an over-zealous soldier wounds Menelaos. During the battle that follows, Diomedes, an Achaian, dominates the action, killing innumerable Trojans and wounding Aphrodite, a goddess.

The Trojans seem to be losing, so Hektor returns to Troy to ask his mother to offer sacrifices to Athena. She performs the rituals, but Athena refuses to accept them. Meanwhile, Hektor discovers Paris safe in his bedroom with Helen, and shames him into returning to battle. Then Hektor visits with his wife and their baby son. It is clear that Hektor is deeply devoted to his family, yet feels the terrible weight of his responsibility as commander-in-chief of the Trojan army.

During the fighting that continues, the Achaians begin to falter, and at one point Athena, Zeus' daughter, fears that the entire Achaian army may be slaughtered. Thus, she and Apollo decide to have Hektor challenge one of the Achaian' warriors to a duel in order to settle the war. Telamonian Aias (Ajax) battles Hektor so valiantly that the contest ends in a draw, and a truce is called.

During this break in the fighting, the dead of both armies are buried and given appropriate funeral rites, and the Achaians fortify their defenses with a strong wall and a moat-like ditch.

The fighting resumes, and so many Achaians are slaughtered that Agamemnon suggests that his troops sail for home, but finally he is convinced that he must return to the fighting. Messengers are sent to Achilles, asking him to return to battle, but Achilles is still sulking beside his ships and refuses to fight.

Soon Agamemnon, Diomedes, Odysseus, and old Nestor are all seriously wounded, and Achilles realizes that the Achaians are in danger of imminent defeat. Therefore, he sends his warrior-companion, Patroklos, to find out who the seriously wounded are.

Patroklos talks with old Nestor, one of the wisest of the Achaian soldiers. Nestor asks Patroklos to dress in Achilles' armor and return to battle. The Achaians, he says, will rejoice and have new faith in their death struggle against the Trojans when they think that they see Achilles returning to the battle. In addition, the Trojans will so fear the wrath of the mighty Achilles that they will be easily defeated. Patroklos promises to ask Achilles for permission to use his armor and ride into battle disguised as the mighty warrior.

Meanwhile, Hektor leads a massive Trojan surge against the Achaian wall that stands between the Trojans and the Achaian fleet of ships, and the wall is successfully smashed. The tumult is so deafening that hell itself seems unloosed.

Achilles is watching and realizes that his wish may be granted: The Achaians are about to be annihilated. He sends Patroklos into the fighting, disguised as Achilles himself. The Achaian army rejoices at what they think is the return of Achilles to the fighting, and the Trojans are so terrified that they are quickly swept back to the walls of Troy.

Patroklos' valor seems superhuman. He has killed nine Trojans in a single charge when Apollo strikes him with such fury that Hektor is able to catch him off-guard and thrust a spear through his body. Then some of the most intense fighting of the war follows in a battle to claim Patroklos' body. Finally, the Achaians rescue Patroklos' corpse, and Hektor captures Achilles' armor. Then the Achaians return to the beach, guarding their ships as best they can.

Achilles is filled with overwhelming grief and rage when he learns that his warrior-companion, Patroklos, has been slaughtered. His mother, Thetis, comes to him and advises him that it is fated that he will die if he tries to revenge Patroklos' death. But she says that if Achilles decides to revenge Patroklos' death, she will outfit him in a suit of new armor, made by one of the gods.

Achilles chooses: He will defy certain death and the Trojans in an attempt to punish them for what they (and he) did to Patroklos. Thus, he returns to battle in his new armor and is so successful that he and the Achaians rout the Trojans. He savagely kills Hektor, the Trojans' mightiest warrior. Achilles' anger is not sated, however. He ties Hektor's corpse to his chariot and circles Patroklos' burial mound every day for nine days.

Hektor's parents are so grieved at the barbaric treatment given to their son's corpse that Priam, Hektor's father, goes to Achilles and begs for his son's body. Achilles is moved by Priam's pleas and by the memory of his own father. Consequently, he agrees to cleanse and return Hektor's body.

Hektor's body is given the appropriate cremation rites, and then with mourning and weeping for the noble warrior, the Trojans place his remains in a golden casket and place it in a burial barrow.

List of Characters

In the *Iliad* certain heroic characters play major roles in the battles even though the reader knows that many more common soldiers must be involved. The heroes, however, are presented literally as greater human beings than the ordinary warriors. Some may have a divine or semi-divine parent, though the hero himself is still mortal and subject to death, unlike the gods. Heroes are of such stature that they sometimes provoke envy from the gods and on occasion may even fight with a god. Each hero is distinguished by a virtue but may also have an accompanying vice. For example, Achilles is the greatest warrior, but he is also petulant and self-centered. In terms of status, heroes are below the gods but above the ordinary warriors.

Overall, heroes lived by four rules: *arete,* the pursuit of excellence, as exemplified by *valor* in battle, and *nobility*, as exemplified by skill in speech and diplomacy. Each of the greatest of these noble heroes is given an *aristeia*, or greatest moment in battle, somewhere in the *Iliad*.

The Achaians: Heroes

Achilles The central character of the *Iliad* and the greatest warrior in the Achaian army. The most significant flaw in the temperament of Achilles is his excessive pride. He is willing to subvert the good of the whole army and to endanger the lives of those who are closest to him to achieve emotional blackmail. Chief virtue: a fighter. His humanity stems from his great passion.

Agamemnon The well-meaning but irresolute king of Mycenae; commander-in-chief of the expedition against Troy. He is a brother of Menelaos. Chief virtue: being a king. His humanity stems from his broad mindedness that makes him a weak king.

Diomedes He ranks among the finest and bravest of the Achaian warriors; he is always wise and reasonable and is renowned for his courtesy and gallantry. He is, perhaps, Homer's vision of the perfect young nobleman. He is sometimes called "lord of the battle cry."

Aias (Ajax) Son of Telamon, he is often called Telamonian Aias; his reputation is due primarily to brute strength and courage, which are his virtues in the poem. Epithet: wall of army.

Odysseus The shrewdest and most subtle of all the Achaians and a brave warrior besides, as he demonstrates on many occasions. Epithet: "Seed of Zeus." Chief virtue: intelligence motivated by persistence, which is his humanity.

Nestor The oldest of the Achaian warriors at Troy. Nestor has all the wisdom and experience of age and is a valuable asset in the council. Although he can no longer fight, he remains at the front line at every battle, commanding his troops. He is often referred to as "Gerenian Nestor."

The Achaians: Warriors

Warriors tend to be somewhat lesser individuals than the heroes are, although still much greater than ordinary men. Their parents are usually mortals, and they are not given *aristeias* in the *Iliad*.

Aias the Lesser A distinguished warrior, but insolent and conceited. He is the son of Oileus and is often called Oilean Aias.

Antilochos The son of Nestor; a brave young warrior who takes an active part in the fighting and the funeral games.

Automedon The squire and charioteer of Achilles.

Helen Originally married to Menelaos, she ran away to Troy with Paris and became his wife. Supposedly, she is the most beautiful woman in the world; however, she is also self-centered.

Idomeneus The King of Crete and one of the most efficient of the Achaian leaders, he has the respect and liking of the whole Achaian army.

Kalchas Soothsayer and prophet of the Achaians.

Menelaos King of Sparta and brother of Agamemnon He was the husband of Helen, who was abducted by Paris.

Patroklos Achilles' close friend and warrior-companion.

The Trojans and their allies: Heroes

Aeneas Son of Aphrodite; a Trojan nobleman. He is second in command of the Trojan army and a brave, skillful warrior.

Hektor Prince of Troy and son of Priam and Hekuba. Hektor is commander of all the Trojan and allied forces. He is the greatest of the Trojan warriors and one of the most noble characters in the *Iliad*. He is always conscious of his duty and his responsibilities to his people and does not let his personal interests interfere. He is a devoted and loving husband and father.

The Trojans and their allies: Warriors

Andromache The wife of Hektor. She seems to illustrate Homer's idea of the good wife and mother; she is loyal, loving, and concerned for her family, and is willing to accept the decisions of her husband.

Antenor A Trojan nobleman who unsuccessfully advocates the return of Helen to the Achaians.

Astyanax The infant son of Hektor and Andromache.

Chryseis Daughter of Chryses, the priest of Apollo. She is the "war prize" hostage of Agamemnon until Apollo demands that she be returned to her father.

Dolon A Trojan nobleman, captured by Odysseus and Diomedes during their night expedition to the Trojan camp in Book X.

Glaukos A prince; a renowned warrior.

Hekuba Wife of Priam. Hektor is the most prominent of her sons.

Helenos Son of Priam and Hekuba; a prince of Troy and a seer.

Cassandra The daughter of Priam and Hekuba; Hektor and Paris' sister.

Pandaros A good archer, but a treacherous man; it is he who breaks the truce in Book IV.

Paris (Alexandros) A prince of Troy; son of Priam and Hekuba; also husband of Helen. He seems content to allow the Trojans to fight for him. He is reprimanded for this by Hektor more than once. His reputation is that of a "pretty boy." His smoothness and glibness are not admired by the warriors of either side, and they often accuse him of cowardice.

Poulydamas One of the Trojan leaders; a very able and clear-headed military strategist whose advice to Hektor is usually not heeded.

Priam King of Troy. He is very old and no longer able to command his army in the field, but his great courage is seen when he travels to the Achaian camp one night to ransom Hektor's body. He is a noble and generous man, one of the few Trojans besides Hektor who treats Helen with respect and courtesy, despite her infidelity to her husband and the war caused by her actions.

The Gods

Gods differ from mortals primarily in their immortality. They are unaware of the fear of death and sometimes seem unable to grasp the pain and horror that fighting and dying bring to mortal warriors. The gods have ichor, an immortal fluid, rather than blood; they eat ambrosia and drink nectar. They live on Mt. Olympos, though in the *Iliad* Zeus often watches the battle from Mt. Ida. The gods can and do change shape and interact with humans. Occasionally, the gods fight humans and suffer wounds, but this doesn't cause the gods any real harm, because the gods cannot bleed or die. The Greek gods are all anthropomorphic: They look like humans, although they are taller, larger, more beautiful, and they often exhibit human emotions such as anger, envy, and deceit.

Zeus The supreme god and king of Olympos. His duty is to carry out the will of Destiny, so he is officially neutral in the war, but he is sympathetic toward the Trojans, particularly Hektor and Priam, and he supports Achilles against Agamemnon. Of all the gods, he alone seems able to change fate, though he chooses not to because of the disruption to the world that would be caused. He is married to Hera with whom he is often in disputes.

Hera Sister and wife of Zeus. She is the most fanatical of all the Olympian supporters of the Achaians and is willing to go to any lengths, including the deception of her husband, to achieve the defeat of Troy. She was the goddess of women and childbirth.

Athena Daughter of Zeus; she sprang directly from his head and became the goddess of wisdom. She plays a prominent role in the war, fighting on the Achaian side. She is also known as the battle goddess and is often referred to as Pallas or Pallas Athena.

Aphrodite Daughter of Zeus; goddess of love and sexual desire. She is the mother of Aeneas and is the patron of Paris, so she fights on

the Trojan side. Her love is Ares, god of war. She is especially con-
nected with Paris and Helen in the *Iliad*.

Apollo Son of Zeus; god of prophecy, light, poetry, and music. He
fights on the Trojan side. Apollo is responsible for the plague in
Book I that leads to the argument between Achilles and
Agamemnon. He is also called Loxias, meaning "tricky."

Ares Son of Zeus and Hera, and the god of war. He is the lover of
Aphrodite and fights on the Trojan side, despite an earlier promise
to Hera and Athena that he would support the Achaians. Only
Aphrodite likes him.

Artemis Daughter of Zeus; sister of Apollo; goddess of chastity,
hunting, and wild animals. She fights on the Trojan side, but with
little effect.

Dione Mother of Aphrodite.

Hades God of the dead and ruler of the underworld.

Hermes Ambassador of the gods; conductor of dead souls to Hades
and a patron of travelers. He is on the Achaians' side, but he does
little to aid them. He escorts Priam on his visit to Achilles in Book
XXIV.

Iris A messenger of the gods.

Poseidon Younger brother of Zeus; god of the sea. He is a strong
supporter of the Achaian cause, having an old grudge against Troy.
He is also somewhat resentful of Zeus' claim to authority over him.

Thetis Mother of Achilles, a sea nymph. She is a staunch advocate
of her son in his quarrel with Agamemnon and does all she can to
help him, but she is not otherwise involved in the war.

Xanthos Son of Zeus; god of one of the major rivers of Troy. He
fights Achilles in Book XXI, but is defeated by Hephaistos' fire.

Character Map

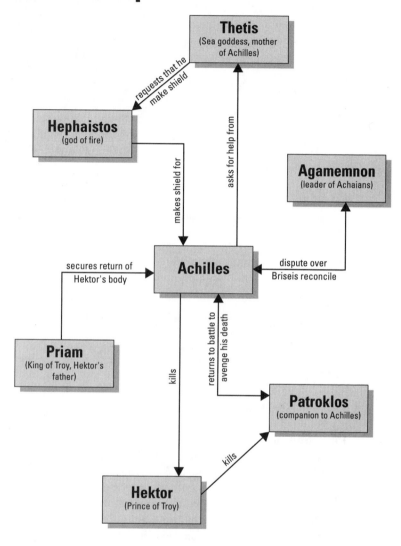

Thetis
(Sea goddess, mother of Achilles)

Hephaistos
(god of fire)

requests that he make shield

asks for help from

makes shield for

Agamemnon
(leader of Achaians)

Achilles

secures return of Hektor's body

dispute over Briseis reconcile

Priam
(King of Troy, Hektor's father)

kills

returns to battle to avenge his death

Patroklos
(companion to Achilles)

Hektor
(Prince of Troy)

kills

CRITICAL COMMENTARIES

Book I

Summary

Chronicling the deeds of great heroes from the past who helped form a society, the *Iliad* is an *epic poem*. As such the epic stands as a bridge between history and literature. As was the tradition in epic poetry, the *Iliad* opens *in medias res*, meaning "in the middle of things," although the action is always preceded by the poet's invocation to the muse (the goddess) of poetry. In this invocation, Homer states his theme—*the wrath, or the anger, of Achilles and its effects*—and requests the aid of the muse so that he can properly recount the story. The reader is then carried to the point where the trouble originally arose, which is where the story of the *Iliad* actually begins: in the middle of war.

During one of the Achaian (Greek) army's many raids on the cities located near Troy, the Achaians captured two beautiful enemy maidens, Chryseis and Briseis. The troops awarded these girls to Agamemnon, the commander-in-chief of the army, and to Achilles, the Achaians' greatest warrior.

Chryses, the father of Chryseis, pleads for her return but Agamemnon denies the plea. Consequently, Chryses prays to Apollo who brings a plague on the Achaian camp. On the tenth day of the plague, Achilles can wait no longer for King Agamemnon to act to end the plague. Usurping Agamemnon's authority, Achilles calls an assembly of the army, and he suggests that a soothsayer be called upon to determine the cause of Apollo's anger. Kalchas, an Achaian soothsayer, volunteers to explain the cause of the pestilence, but only if he is guaranteed personal protection. Achilles agrees to this condition.

When the soothsayer reveals that the plague is the result of Agamemnon's refusal to return Chryseis to her father, Agamemnon is furious that he has been publicly named as being responsible for the plague. He insists that *if he is forced* to surrender Chryseis, his rightful war prize, then he *must be repaid* with Achilles' war prize, Briseis.

However, Achilles is stunned by the public disgrace of having Agamemnon demand Briseis, and he refuses to accept the indignity that he feels Agamemnon has made him undergo in full view of all the soldiers. Thus, he announces that he is withdrawing all of his troops from battle. He will *not* fight, and, furthermore, he and his men will return to their own country as soon as possible.

Nevertheless, Agamemnon decides to appease Apollo; he will return Chryseis, his war prize. He sends her safely aboard a ship heading home, and then he sends his heralds to collect Briseis (Achilles' war prize) for him. Surprisingly, Achilles surrenders the girl without any difficulty.

Achilles, in despair, prays to his mother, Thetis, the sea-goddess asking her to use her influence with Zeus to ensure that the Trojan armies defeat his fellow Achaian soldiers. Achilles hopes that this result will cause disgrace for Agamemnon and so repay the wrong that the King did to Achilles.

Thetis visits Zeus on Olympos, and the king of the gods agrees to aid the Trojans, although he expresses a fear that his wife, Hera, will be annoyed because she is jealous of Thetis and hates the Trojans and hence cannot bear to see them win the war. Readers discover that Hera does indeed hate the Trojans, but she fears Zeus' wrath even more, and so she quiets her protests. The first book ends with a banquet of the gods in Zeus' palace.

Commentary

In Book I, the initial quarrel between Agamemnon and Achilles, mediated by Nestor, is paralleled at the end of the book by the quarrel between Zeus and Hera, mediated by Hephaistos. The quarrel among the gods breaks down into a humorous scene that ironically accentuates the seriousness of the human quarrel. Homer's technique of repeating an earlier scene with a later one is used throughout the *Iliad*. In fact, this structural technique is a basis for the entire work. However, Book I essentially sets up the tension for the rest of the poem. The wrath of Achilles seems justified from Book I to Book IX. Achilles' wrath is held up for criticism from Book IX to Book XVIII. And finally there is reconciliation in Books XVIII and XIX. This pattern repeats in Books XIX through XXIV. Achilles wrath is justifiable in Book XIX to Book XXII. His wrath is criticized in Books XXII to Book XXIV. And finally, there is reconciliation in Book XXIV when Achilles and Priam meet.

Book I opens with the words, "Rage—Goddess, sing the rage of Peleus' son Achilles." Homer invokes the muse ("Goddess") of epic poetry to aid him in telling the story of Achilles' anger and the great war for Helen and Troy. He further introduces in the word "rage" one of the human qualities, along with pride and honor, that will make up a major theme of the work as a whole. Initially, Achilles' anger seems a reasonable response to the arrogance of Agamemnon, but as the poem progresses, it becomes clear that righteous anger can degenerate into petty resentment or escalate into uncontrollable rage. The necessity for reason and self-control over emotions becomes an overriding idea in the *Iliad.*

Similarly, the related concepts of pride and honor are introduced in Book I. Both Agamemnon and Achilles believe that their honor is compromised in the decisions involving the female captives, Chryseis and Briseis. Pride and honor were important principles to the Greeks, particularly because those traits involved public perception. Agamemnon thinks that Achilles, by calling the council and demanding that Chryseis be returned to Chryses, has challenged his leadership and impugned his honor. Likewise, Achilles feels that Agamemnon's decision to take Briseis as a replacement for Chryseis is an affront to his honor and a public show of disrespect by the Achaian leader. Individual senses of pride and honor here blind the two warriors to the greater good. Their *hubris*— overweening pride—requires them to react in foolish ways, Agamemnon in taking Achilles' captive Briseis and Achilles in withdrawing himself and his troops from battle. Homer once again shows that a noble human trait can be subverted by emotion into pettiness and irrationality.

However, Achilles' decision to withdraw appears much more reasonable in Book I than it will later in the poem. From Book I to Book IX, Achilles' anger and withdrawal from battle seem to have some justification. He retains the reader's sympathy even though his decisions seem to be overreactions.

A second theme introduced in Book I is the nature of the relationship between the gods and men. When Agamemnon refuses to give up Chryseis, Chryses prays to Apollo, who comes down to devastate the Achaians with his arrows, a symbolic representation of plague. Later, angered by Agamemnon, Achilles starts to draw his sword to kill the Achaian leader. Athena intervenes and calms the overwrought Achilles, a symbolic representation of reason controlling the will. Finally, Thetis, Achilles' goddess mother, goes to Zeus to ask for punishment on Agamemnon and the Achaians for their actions against her son. Zeus nods in agreement, thereby initiating the series of Trojan triumphs that make up much of the first half of the work. Zeus' decision leads to a quarrel among the gods that humorously reflects the quarrel among the Greeks.

Homer shows the gods in a variety of relationships with humans. First, in the instances of the destruction caused by Apollo and the forbearance produced by Athena, Homer is using the gods as dramatic, almost allegoric causes for natural events and actions. Second, just as clearly, he also shows that the gods take an active role in human affairs. Apollo and Zeus both mete out a kind of rough justice, a justice that seems in both cases much harsher than the offense warranted. Third, the intervention of the gods also suggests an interrelationship between humans and gods that is related to the fate of humans. At times, characters such as Achilles seem to have free will. At other times, the gods seem to control the destiny of humans. And, at other times, neither gods nor men seem to be in control of human fate—it simply is what it is.

In the past few decades, some psychological studies have suggested a different approach to the god/human relationships in the *Iliad.* An entirely different approach to the god and human relationship has been offered by psychologist Julian Jaynes in *The Origin of Consciousness in the Breakdown of the Bicameral Mind* (Houghton Mifflin, 1990). Jaynes presents the idea that modern consciousness is of relatively recent origin and that earlier man had a bicameral mind, one chamber of which literally spoke to the other when decisions or thoughtful action was needed. Jaynes sees the *Iliad* as a book dealing with pre-modern minds. Therefore, when Athena tells Achilles not to draw his sword to kill Agamemnon, the speaker is actually one side of Achilles' brain. Jaynes idea accounts for the intervention of the gods as a way in which these early men accounted for the voices they heard within their own brains.

Glossary

Kalchas Greek prophet or seer. Originally told Agamemnon that he must sacrifice Iphigeneia for Greeks to be able to sail to Troy. Tells Agamemnon that Chryseis must be returned to her father.

Hephaistos Greek God of Fire and Forge; compare to Vulcan in Roman mythology.

Muses nine goddesses, daughters of Zeus, who preside over various art forms. Homer invokes the Muse of Epic Poetry.

Ocean River the Greeks conceived of the ocean as a river rising in the west and encircling the world.

Peleus father of Achilles; King of the Myrmidons.

Phoebus One of several names of Apollo.

scepter a rod or staff, highly ornamented, held by rulers on ceremonial occasions as a symbol of sovereignty. The passing of the scepter to a person by the herald indicated permission to speak.

Smintheus another name, or epithet, for Apollo. This title is often translated as "Mouse God" and relates to Apollo's role in the plague in Book I.

Thetis sea goddess, daughter of Nereus; immortal mother of Achilles.

Book II

Summary

Zeus, fulfilling his promise to Thetis that he will help the Trojans, sends a fraudulent dream of hope to Agamemnon. Agamemnon is absolutely convinced by his dream that he can defeat the Trojans once and for all in battle the next morning. So, full of false hope, he and his council plan a mass assault on Troy.

But, to test the loyalty of his army before he begins this mass assault, Agamemnon announces to the soldiers that nine years of war is more than enough; they should return home. To his great surprise, his troops react to his suggestion with loud enthusiasm. Breaking ranks, they run to prepare their ships for the trip home. Only through the efforts of Odysseus, guided by Athena, is the mad rush to the ships halted. Then Odysseus convinces the Achaians that it is far more honorable to remain and conquer Troy. Wise old Nestor adds his voice to that of Odysseus, and the army agrees to stay and fight.

Offering a sacrifice to Zeus, Agamemnon orders the army to prepare itself for the attack. He then holds a splendid review of the whole Achaian army, thus giving Homer an opportunity to enumerate all of the Achaian contingents and their heroes.

When news of the Achaian maneuver is received in Troy, Hektor orders his troops to prepare to meet the Achaians on the plain in front of Troy. Then, as the Trojan troops march through the city gates, Homer gives us a review of the Trojan leaders and the cities that have sent military assistance to them.

Commentary

Book II is divided into two large segments: Agamemnon's dream and the rallying of the men after they try to return to the ships, and the great catalogue of the Greek kings, heroes, and ships that have come to Troy.

The catalogue is a significant break in the action of the epic, serving as a list of all the characters involved in the rest of the poem as well as a reminder that eight years of fighting have preceded the opening of this story. The catalogue is also of interest to historians and other scholars who use its descriptions of over 150 places and characters as a source for piecing together information about Bronze Age Greece.

Analysis of the information found in these two catalogues of opposing armies has been of great value to historians, linguists, and archaeologists in reconstructing an important and little-known period of early Greek history. The presence of these catalogues in the *Iliad* is a good example of the way Homer composed his poems on a foundation of historical and literary tradition.

The first part of Book II involves the false dream that Zeus sends to Agamemnon. In this instance, the god does not advise or aid the human, but actually deceives him in an effort to inflict injury on the Greeks. There is more than a hint in Zeus' use of this false dream that he thinks he can overcome fate and be able to prevent the victory of the Greeks over the Trojans. More obviously, Zeus' intervention shows that the gods are not always concerned with the consequences their actions may have on the humans. The false dream causes death and destruction for both Greeks and Trojans, but that fact does not enter into of Zeus' thinking. That humans are mortal is of little importance to the immortal gods.

Agamemnon's reaction to the dream further calls into question his adequacy as a leader. First, he accepts the dream without question. Second, he decides to test his men's desire for battle by offering them the prospect of returning home instead of continuing in the war. To men who have been away from home, wives, and children for more than eight years, the offer seems to be worth far more than glory and honor, and a near riot of men rushing to the ships ensues. Third, it is not Agamemnon but Odysseus and Nestor who bring the men's hearts and minds back to war and personal honor.

This issue of war and men's honor is brought into distinct focus through the speech of Thersites and Odysseus' response to it. Thersites, a physically misshapen Greek warrior, argues forcefully and effectively that the war is not worth fighting and that Agamemnon is a flawed leader, constantly taking the largest share of loot for himself and having now alienated Achilles in the process. His argument, strong as it is, is no match for the verbal attack that Odysseus makes on Thersites. Odysseus makes the point that Thersites is a commoner and has no business speaking out against kings and nobles. Odysseus further implies that Thersites has no personal pride or honor because he does not wish to fight. Also, Thersites' lack of honor is reinforced symbolically by his deformed appearance. Odysseus punctuates his attack by slapping Thersites on the back with a scepter, raising a welt and causing tears to flow. This public humiliation and marking of Thersites ends all talk of returning home. Pride and honor require soldiers to fight. Only the deformed in mind and body would argue otherwise.

Literary Device

Also in Book II, Homer begins to utilize the *epic* or *extended simile* more frequently. These similes are used throughout the work more frequently than the more common simple simile. For example, in line 544 Homer compares the armies to "flocks of winging birds, geese or cranes," and then adds the specific appearance of the birds and the precise place—"round the Cayster outflow"—where the birds flock. Other such similes may extend to a page or more in length. These similes, when examined, add much detail and comment on the individual scenes in which they occur. Analysis of specific similes produces a deeper understanding of the work as a whole.

Glossary

aegis a shield borne by Zeus and later, by his daughter Athena and occasionally by Apollo; a sign of Zeus' protection.

Catalogue of Ships list of Greek kings and their countries in Book II. This listing of a group of warriors, countries, or other items is a relatively common epic device.

epic simile a simile is a comparison using *like* or *as*. An *epic simile* is an extended simile that may go on for ten, twenty, or more lines and may contain multiple points of comparison.

epithets a descriptive name or title. Phrases such as "breaker of horses," "long-haired," or "well-greaved," are frequently associated with a particular character or sometimes warrior group. The epithet was an epic device or convention that helped the poet in the oral composition process.

Mycenae Achaian kingdom of Agamemnon. Mycenae was probably the most famous of all the Greek kingdoms.

Thersites Greek soldier who verbally criticizes Agamemnon. He is ugly and somewhat deformed and treated as a comic character. He is the only common soldier to have a speaking role in the *Iliad*. He is put down both verbally and physically by Odysseus.

Book III

Summary

The two armies advance, and as they draw toward each other, Paris (the warrior who kidnapped Menelaos' wife, Helen) brashly steps forward and dares any of the Achaian warriors to meet him in personal combat. The challenge is eagerly accepted by Menelaos, but Paris is suddenly overcome by terror and hides within the Trojan ranks.

Hektor, the Trojan commander, finds his brother Paris and gives him a stern tongue-lashing. Paris is so ashamed that he agrees to a duel with Menelaos. A truce is declared while Agamemnon and Hektor determine the conditions of the duel, and it is arranged that Paris (Helen's lover) and Menelaos (Helen's husband) will engage in single combat. The victor will win Helen, and a treaty of peace will be agreed upon, after which the Achaians will sail for home.

Meanwhile, back in Troy, King Priam and his council sit on the ramparts watching the battlefield. Helen is with them, and she identifies the Achaian commanders for him and tells him a little about their deeds. While the two discuss the Achaians, Priam is called to the field to give his consent to the terms of the truce. When he arrives, he joins his arch-enemy, Agamemnon, in a sacrifice to the gods on behalf of both armies; then they solemnize the agreement. Afterward, Priam returns to Troy while Paris and Menelaos prepare to fight.

The duel is fought with javelin and sword in a large open area between the two armies. Menelaos is the superior warrior, and he inflicts a slight wound on Paris. The Trojan prince is taken captive, but while Menelaos is dragging him to the Achaian lines, Aphrodite intervenes and rescues her favorite warrior. She conceals him "in a thick mist" and carries him off to his bedroom in Troy, where she brings Helen to him.

Agamemnon steps to the front of his army and states that the duel has unquestionably been won by Menelaos, and he demands the immediate restoration of Helen. The Achaians loudly applaud the decision of their king and commander-in-chief.

Commentary

Literary
Device

Structurally, Book III follows a pattern that Homer uses many times in the *Iliad*—one scene is followed by a second that reflects the first and reinforces ideas within it. In Book III the war between the Greeks and the Trojans is personified in the hand-to-hand duel between Menelaos and Paris—the two men whose dispute over Helen is the cause of the entire war. Their fight is symbolically between the warrior (Menelaos) and the lover (Paris). Menelaos wins the battle, but Paris, whisked away to the bedroom by Aphrodite, wins the girl.

This conflict between Menelaos and Paris re-emerges in the second scene of the Book as Helen attempts to reject Paris for Menelaos. Helen announces that she will have nothing more to do with Paris, but when Aphrodite, who symbolizes Helen's carnal nature, threatens her, Helen immediately gives in and goes to bed with Paris. Homer frequently associates the qualities of a god with a character or an action in the poem. That Helen and Paris are overcome with carnal passion represented by Aphrodite and her threats is quite plain here. Helen would like to choose the honorable warrior, Menelaos, but her sexuality and passion control her and she returns to the bed of Paris, who is also unable to control his passionate nature and complete his battle with Menelaos. As Helen and Paris make love, Menelaos rages on the battlefield looking for the man he thought he had defeated. The skillful structuring of sections of the *Iliad*, such as in Book III, suggests that a single author lay behind the composition of the poem.

Book III makes it clear that human passion must be controlled if men are to be successful. By fighting with Menelaos and abiding by the terms of the truce, Paris could end the war that his actions caused. However, Paris can no more control his passion than Helen can control hers. In fact, Paris does not even try. He leaves the battlefield and glory albeit that glory on the battlefield is death, to make love with Helen. Just as Agamemnon and Achilles cannot control their pride and anger, so Paris cannot control his lust. Pride, anger, honor, passion— all these human traits, Homer suggests, must be brought under control if men are to succeed. Book III shows, through Paris and Helen, how lack of control has terrible consequences. Because he cannot control his lust, Paris causes the war to rage on more fiercely than ever. In contrast, Odysseus, the one Greek who uses reason to control his emotions, ultimately devises the plan that ends the war.

Character Insight

The introduction of Helen in this book and the images associated with her emphasize the sexuality inherent in her nature. When first encountered by the reader, Helen is weaving a tapestry, much like Penelope in the *Odyssey*. The tapestry depicts the course of the war, and while on one level it represents a kind of occupational therapy for Helen as she awaits the outcome, on another level it suggests that she is the weaver or cause of the war. Her physical beauty is never described, but the admiration of the old Trojans before they go to make the truce with Agamemnon makes her desirability clearer than any attempt at literal description.

Glossary

Antenor one of the Trojan elders; advises Priam.

Crete island in the Mediterranean Sea south of Greece. Legendary home of King Minos, the labyrinth, and the Minotaur. In the *Iliad*, it is the kingdom of Idomeneus.

greaves armor for the leg from the ankle to the knee worn by Homeric warriors.

Iris messenger goddess, usually for Zeus.

Scaean Gate the main gates of the city of Troy.

shield a flat, usually broad, piece of metal or wood carried in the hand or worn on the forearm to ward off blows or missiles. The shields used by Homeric warriors could be the small, round, metal buckler or the larger, oval, ox-hide constructions that protected the entire body.

spear a weapon consisting of a long wooden shaft with a sharp point, usually of metal or stone, for thrusting or throwing. The Homeric warriors fight mainly with a large thrusting spear that is sometimes thrown. Swords, bows, and arrows are less frequently used.

Book IV

Summary

The gods meet in conference on Olympos. Zeus proposes that because Menelaos has obviously won the duel, the long, nine-year war be brought to a close. Hera and Athena dislike this course of action, and Hera, in particular, vehemently protests to Zeus. She wants the complete destruction of Troy, a city she bitterly hates. She wants no truce. Zeus gives in and sends Athena to somehow arrange a resumption of the fighting.

At Troy, Athena seeks out Pandaros, one of the Trojan leaders, and tempts him to kill Menelaos, thereby gaining great glory. Pandaros foolishly acts on her advice and draws his bow, as the truce is still in effect. He shoots an arrow at Menelaos, but Athena makes sure that it *only* *wounds* Menelaos because she doesn't want him dead, but she does want the battle to begin anew. Agamemnon and the Achaians are shocked by this violation of the truce and by the seemingly serious injury to Menelaos. Fortunately, the wound is not fatal, but while an army surgeon is treating it, several of the Trojan regiments begin to advance suddenly in battle order.

Agamemnon immediately orders his troops to prepare to fight, and he goes through the ranks of his army, praising the men. The Achaians respond to their king's spirit and they eagerly and cheerfully arm themselves and fall into line. The war begins again. The two armies clash violently, and large numbers of men on both sides are killed.

Commentary

Book IV begins with an argument among the gods in which Zeus taunts Hera and Athena about the possibility of ending the war at once because Paris has lost the duel with Menelaos. However, after Hera's impassioned argument against the Trojans, Zeus immediately sends Athena to trick Pandaros. Pandaros, referred to as a "fool" for being taken in by Athena, breaks the truce and attempts to kill Menelaos with an arrow. These two scenes—the argument and attack—are followed by parallel scenes among the Greeks. Agamemnon reviews his troops, taunting or praising the warriors as he thinks best. He is similar to a modern football coach "psyching up" individual players in different ways before the game. Agamemnon's attitude toward his warriors is similar to Zeus' attitude toward the other gods. His comments are intended to produce a particular response. Zeus mocks another god to produce a particular reaction. Agamemnon criticizes or praises based on his assessment of the warrior's personality. After the review, the first major battle scene of the *Iliad* begins.

The significant comparison between the scenes involving the gods and those involving Agamemnon and the troops is that for the gods, their decisions are almost jokes; Zeus can mock Hera and Athena even though he knows that he will send Athena to Pandaros and that the war will continue. In contrast, for Agamemnon and the soldiers, the taunting and the fighting are matters of life and death, of individual and collective survival.

The significance of Pandaros' shot at Menelaos should not be overlooked; it is a crucial moment in the epic. If Pandaros does not take the shot, the war could end. To accentuate the importance of the moment, Homer describes the bow and the shot in extended detail. Such involved descriptions of weaponry are common in both the *Iliad* and the *Odyssey*. The technique is also used in later epics, such as the long histories of the swords in the great Anglo-Saxon epic *Beowulf*.

Humor in the *Iliad* is most often associated with the gods but does occasionally show up among the humans, most often in connection with Nestor. In Book IV, however, Agamemnon's reaction to Menelaos' flesh wound is humorous. Agamemnon, seeing blood, thinks that his brother has been mortally wounded and begins a long speech of lament and revenge, concluding with the idea that eventually he will return to Greece "leaving behind the hero Menelaos/ mouldering in his wake." Menelaos undercuts Agamemnon's oration by saying that he is not really hurt. Agamemnon's concern for his brother may be genuine, but he comes across as overprotective.

Finally, the graphic nature of the battle scenes startle some first-time readers, but the straightforward nature of these depictions is part of Homer's technique. The description of wounds and death may be realistic, but the actual battle descriptions are stylized, examples of the set pieces used in epic composition (see Introduction). Examples of this stylized description are phrases such as, "the sound of struggle roared and rocked the earth," "rushing madly to strip his gear," or "loosed his limbs." Homer understandably focuses on individual combat of heroes while ignoring the multitude of foot soldiers who must have borne the brunt of the fighting. The gods, representing elemental forces and passions, help both sides.

Glossary

Aias the Greek forces in the *Iliad* have two Aiases (also known as Ajax). The stronger and more prominent one is Telamonian Aias, King from Salamis. He is a notable fighter often referred to as the Great Aias. Oilean Aias is from Locris and is sometimes called Little Aias.

breastplate a piece of armor for the breast.

Chiron wise centaur (part horse, part human) who taught Achilles.

Machaon son of the famous healer Asclepius. Machaon is from Thessalia and is often used as a healer in the *Iliad*.

wall Troy is a fortress, surrounded by an almost impregnable wall of stone that Poseidon helped construct. The Greeks made a wall of rocks, sand, and wood to protect their ships. The Greek wall is the one most often referred to in the *Iliad*.

Book V

Summary

The battle continues with great fury, and both armies perform many acts of valor. During this particular day's fighting, the outstanding warrior is Diomedes, whom the goddess Athena has inspired with exceptional courage and skill.

When Pandaros (who wounded Menelaos) wounds Diomedes, the valiant Achaian soldier appeals to Athena for aid. She answers him by giving him additional courage, plus the privilege of *being able to distinguish gods from men*. She warns him, however, *not* to fight against any of the gods—with the exception of Aphrodite.

Diomedes returns to the front line and drives the Trojans back before him. He kills many Trojans, including Pandaros, and then he wounds Aeneas, the son of the goddess Aphrodite. Diomedes takes the splendid horses of Aeneas as a war prize and is about to finish off Aeneas himself when Aphrodite comes down to protect her son. Enraged at Aphrodite's interference, Diomedes pursues her and wounds her in the hand. With tears streaming down her face, Aphrodite flees in terror to Olympos and seeks solace from Dione, her mother. Zeus is angry at this turn of events and orders Aphrodite to stay off the battlefield in the future because warfare is *not* the same as love, her usual sphere of interest. Meanwhile, Apollo carries Aeneas off to safety in the temple at Pergamos.

Ares, the savage god of war, enters the Trojan ranks and helps Hektor rally his forces. With his aid, Hektor and the Trojan army again attempt to advance. But the Achaians, led by Diomedes and other Achaian heroes, are able to hold their ground. As the bloody battle progresses, however, the strong and brutal influence of Ares is felt, and the Achaians gradually begin to withdraw toward their camp.

Hera and Athena then fly to the aid of the Achaians, after gaining permission from Zeus to bring Ares under control. On the plains before Troy, Hera gives fresh strength to the Achaians while Athena brings the now-wounded Diomedes back to the fray. She advises him to have no fear of

Ares or any other god. Diomedes gallops into combat, encounters Ares, and drives a spear into his belly. With a bellow of pain and fury, Ares leaves the field and heads for Olympos.

Finding Zeus, Ares complains about the harsh treatment he has received, but the god of war gets no sympathy from Zeus. Zeus tells him that because of his quarrelsome and cruel nature, he has no love for him, but because he is a god, his wound will heal. Athena and Hera then return to the Olympian palace, and the battle between the Achaians and the Trojans continues to rage, but now there are *no gods* fighting on either side.

Commentary

The *aristeia* of a warrior is defined simply as that warrior's greatest battle, the battle in which he reaches his peak as a fighter and hero. Throughout the *Iliad*, many of the characters have aristeias; Book V is the aristeia of Diomedes.

Literary
Device

Book V, sometimes referred to as the *Diomedia*, has its own internal unity and may once have constituted an independent poem, or bardic lay, about the exploits of the Achaian hero Diomedes, which was adapted by Homer and included in the *Iliad.* The long account of the deeds of Diomedes has little to do with the main plot of the *Iliad* in any direct sense and could easily have been omitted or given in less detail, but it has several important artistic functions. Diomedes is a heroic Achaian figure, comparable to Achilles in prowess, gallantry, courage, and divine favor, but with the significant difference that he is *always* courteous, self-controlled, and respectful, even when in dispute with his king, Agamemnon. The tale of Diomedes presents an alternative model of a hero with whom to compare Achilles and by which to judge Achilles' defection from the army during the heat of battle. Diomedes has no more reason to fight for Menelaos than Achilles has. Diomedes has not received war prizes that equal those of Agamemnon or Achilles. Yet when battle arises and he is called upon to do his duty, Diomedes fights with unmatched intensity. Achilles sits in his tent. Additionally, the *Diomedia* is the first and most impressive of the long series of battle scenes and scenes of personal combat that now follow in the absence of Achilles.

Beginning with the high point of Diomedes' heroism, the Achaian successes will now steadily deteriorate into two culminating disasters: Achilles' rejection of Agamemnon's attempt at reconciliation (Book IX) and the Trojans' breaking through the Achaian wall protecting the Achaian ships (Book XII).

Aeneas, one of the Trojan heroes who appears in this book, was in later times claimed by the Romans as their legendary ancestor, and he became the hero of the *Aeneid*, a Classical Latin epic by the poet Virgil. The *Aeneid* chronicles the founding of Rome.

Aphrodite also joins in the fighting in this book, revealing her partisanship for the Trojans. She stands in contrast to Hera and Athena who favor the Achaians. Aphrodite sides with the Trojans because of Paris who had selected her as the most beautiful goddess (see Background to the Epic). Her entry into the battle here also connects her with Aeneas, who is her son.

That gods and goddesses enter the battle is an example of the anthropomorphic nature of Greek gods. That is, they have human shapes, emotions, and other qualities. Aphrodite's concern for her son and her favoritism toward the Trojans are her obvious motivations in entering the battle. Zeus generally tries to keep the gods out of the battle, though this effort often proves futile.

Glossary

Aeneas Trojan warrior, son of Anchises and Aphrodite. In legend, he is the only major Trojan warrior to escape from Troy.

aristeia the greatest battle of a hero. For example, Diomedes' aristeia occurs in Book V; Achilles' aristeia ends the *Iliad*.

brazen made of brass or bronze.

car chariot.

ichor the ethereal fluid flowing instead of blood in the veins of the gods.

Scamander river that flows through the plain on which Troy is located.

Book VI

Summary

The battle continues, and although the gods are no longer taking part, the Achaians drive back the Trojans. There is much slaughter, and in their ardor to defeat the Trojans, the Achaians do not even pause to collect loot.

The Trojan force is in full retreat when Helenos, a soothsayer, suggests that his brother Hektor return to Troy and arrange for the queen and the other royal women of the city to make an offering in the temple of Athena in hopes of placating the goddess. Hektor agrees to the wisdom of this plan, and while he goes back to Troy, there is a short lull in the fighting.

During this interval, Agamemnon orders Menelaos to kill Adrestus even though Menelaos' intends to spare the Trojan. Diomedes and Glaukos step into the area between the two resting armies and challenge each other to personal combat. They discover, however, while explaining their individual pedigrees, that there were once ties of friendship between their grandfathers; thus, according to the heroic code, they *must* maintain these same bonds of friendship. They promise to avoid fighting each other in the battles to come, and, as a token of their fellowship, they trade armor. Diomedes comes out ahead in this exchange because his bronze armor is worth only nine oxen, while the golden armor of Glaukos is worth one hundred oxen, but the two men part as comrades.

In Troy, Hektor instructs his mother, Hekuba, about the rites to be held in Athena's temple, and then he goes to find Paris, who has been absent from the battlefield. He discovers his brother at home with Helen and her handmaidens, and he sternly rebukes him for his irresponsibility. Paris admits that he has been disgracing himself, and he prepares himself to join the fight. Hektor, meanwhile, goes to visit his own wife and baby son.

He finds Andromache and the baby Astyanax on the walls overlooking the battlefield. Andromache pleads with Hektor not to endanger himself any longer. Achilles has killed her father and all her brothers, and now Hektor is her whole family; she begs him to have pity on her and their infant child.

Hektor admits his concern for Andromache, but he says that he must consider his reputation and his duty. In his heart, he says, he knows that Troy *will* fall someday, but he is, after all, foremost a soldier and a prince, and he has many responsibilities. He adds that he often worries about the fate of his dear wife and son after he is dead and his city has been captured, but that a mortal *cannot* change the will of the gods. After saying this, Hektor kisses Andromache and Astyanax and leaves. Paris joins him at the city gate, and they both return to the battlefield.

Commentary

The fighting that began in Book V continues in Book VI. In the overall structure of the epic, this fighting involves three large movements between the ships and the city. These movements end in Books XV, XVI, and XVII when the Trojans fire the Greek ships, Patroklos is killed, and Achilles decides to re-enter the battle.

Within Book VI a distinctive movement from cold-heartedness to tenderness, from barbarity to honor occurs. The opening savagery is represented by Agamemnon, who forces Menelaos to kill the prisoner Adrestus, saying, "No baby boy, still in his mother's belly,/not even he escape." For Agamemnon, there can be no human feelings for the enemy in war.

Agamemnon's brutality is immediately contrasted with the kinship discovered by Glaukos and Diomedes. The two warriors discover that they have ties because of their forebears. They not only pledge friendship but exchange armor as well. The exchange of armor is especially significant because armor was associated with identity, and the exchange is a symbolic exchange of character. In this example, Homer shows that war can entail more than carnage, and that bonds of friendship can be established.

An interesting sideline in this scene is Glaukos' mention of symbols inscribed "on a folded tablet." This example is the only reference to writing in the *Iliad*.

Literary Device

But Homer goes on to show even greater humanity in wartime. As Hektor returns to Troy, he first meets the wives of the Trojan warriors, reminding the reader that for each soldier there is an individual life and story within the city. Likewise, when Hektor sees his mother, Hekuba, their meeting, too, is a reminder of the ties of kinship and love that implicitly exist for every character in the story. Moreover, these ties of love and kinship have all become disconnected by the war. The scenes in Book VI graphically remind the reader why the Greek soldiers rushed to their ships to return home in Book II when they were offered the opportunity to return home.

Before Hektor is reunited with Andromache, he encounters Paris and Helen. Hektor's anger toward Paris is palpable. Paris and Helen are the causes of the war that men such as Hektor and the husbands of the Trojan wives are fighting, while Paris himself lies in bed with Helen. The contrast between the responsible Hektor and the irresponsible Paris is obvious.

This contrast is carried further when Helen makes an oblique pass at Hektor. Hektor tactfully rebuffs her, saying, "Don't ask me to sit beside you here, Helen." Hektor controls his lust and passion even when tempted by Helen. Once again, the contrast with Paris is clear.

The end of Book VI is the famous scene between Hector and Andromache and their infant son, Astyanax. Most commentators consider this scene to be the most moving in the *Iliad*. It is a portrait of the warrior at home, war forgotten as he watches his son play and talks with his wife. Hektor's family becomes a symbol for all the soldier's families, what their lives could be if there were no war. Once again, Hektor is the perfect contrast to Achilles. As Hektor stands in the loving circle of his home and family, Achilles, alienated and alone, rages in his tent. Achilles is more dangerous, but Hektor is more human. In fact, with Hector and Achilles, Homer provides two different paradigms. Both are great warriors, both are destined to die; and yet they represent entirely different value systems. Achilles is the warrior; Hektor the family man. Achilles embodies the values of the individual who fights only for glory and honor; Hektor symbolizes the larger concerns of friends, of family, of home and civilization itself.

However, Homer makes it clear that both Hektor and Achilles are alike in one respect—they will fight and die for honor over all else. Home, family, peace—all mean everything to Hektor, yet he will return to the battle, knowing he will be killed, because honor demands it. Even Paris is roused to leave Helen when his honor is challenged. Similarly, Achilles goes into battle later, knowing he too will die, but feeling that honor requires his presence. Hektor and Achilles are worthy counterparts with different values in most respects, but ultimately alike in their deepest motivations. In the end though, both subscribe to the code that the ultimate honor for a hero is to die in battle.

Glossary

Bellerophon hero from Corinth who killed the Chimaera.

bravado blustering, swaggering conduct; the pretense of bravery. Much of the boasting in battle is a type of bravado.

Chimaera a monster with a lion's head, a snake's tail, and a goat's body, killed by Bellerophon.

distaff a staff on which fibers, such as flax or wool, are wound before being spun into thread.

loom a machine for weaving thread or yarn into cloth. Both the distaff and loom are associated with women in the *Iliad*.

Maenad a female votary of Dionysus who took part in the wild, orgiastic rites that characterized his worship; bacchante.

Book VII and Book VIII

Summary

Book VII

Hektor and Paris rejoin the Trojan forces, and the battle begins again. Athena and Apollo, after witnessing the continued slaughter, decide to end the day's combat by arranging a duel between Hektor and one of the best Achaian warriors. The time consumed by this duel will result in a recess for both armies.

The Greeks cast lots and Telamonian Aias is chosen as the Achaian champion. He and Hektor engage in a ferocious duel, but neither warrior is able to overcome the other. Finally, because it is growing dark, the two men are parted by heralds, and they exchange gifts as tokens of their respective valor.

That night, each of the armies has a feast celebrating the safe return of its champion. In the Achaian camp, Nestor proposes that a short truce be arranged so that funerals for the dead can be held; he also wants to use this time for his fellow Achaians to build a wall and a trench to defend their ships.

In Troy that same evening, one of the Trojan noblemen, Antenor, suggests that Helen be returned to Menelaos. Paris refuses to give up his new wife, but he offers to restore all of Helen's property to Menelaos, plus some of his own as an indemnity. Wise old Priam, Hektor's father, sends a messenger to Agamemnon with this proposition, as well as a request for a truce during which the Trojans can bury their dead. The Achaians refuse the offer by Paris, but both sides agree on the truce.

The next morning, the two armies collect their dead and conduct the funeral rites. At a council on Olympos, Zeus warns the gods that he is at last planning to bring the Trojan War to a finish and that any interference in favor of either side will be punished severely. However, when Athena asks to be allowed to advise the Achaians, Zeus consents.

Book VIII

In the morning, the Trojan forces come out of the city and the armies clash again. Zeus watches over the fighting from nearby Mount Ida and decides to give the day's victory to Troy. A furious battle ensues, and soon the Achaians are driven from the field in complete disorder. Most of the commanders flee also, and old Nestor is saved from Hektor's spear only by the courage of Diomedes.

Hera, who has always been a fanatical hater of the Trojans, tries to convince Poseidon to join her in helping the Achaians. The sea god, however refuses.

Hektor is everywhere, fighting bravely and cheering on his men. Hera and Athena prepare to intervene, but Zeus notices their approach. He repeats his earlier warning through his messenger, Iris, and the goddesses return to Olympos. Meanwhile, the Achaian forces are driven back behind the fortifications protecting their ships.

Hektor orders his army to camp on the plain for the night to prevent the Achaians from sailing off to safety in the darkness and to retain the advantage for the morning's assault. Supplies are brought from Troy, and the Trojan fires burn in front of the Achaian wall.

Commentary

Book VII

Most of Books VII and VIII involve battles, such as the duel between Hektor and Aias at the center of Book VII and the renewed but brief battle that is the subject of Book VIII. A number of incidents make up a typical duel such as the duel between Hektor and Aias. Each of these characteristics may not be in every duel, but all of them are so typical that they may have been part of the mnemonic material that poets fell back on during their recitations.

Before fighting, the combatants may establish their own lineage and then taunt the opponent. This type of speech is not unlike contemporary "trash talk" in sports. After the initial sparring, the battle is described in detail with each spear thrust and parry explained. Wounds are described graphically and with clear anatomical references, including the exact cause of death. Sometimes a dying warrior has final words while the victor often exults over the body. The armor of the dead warrior is removed and claimed by the victor, a symbolic taking of identity. In Book XVII, Hektor actually puts on the armor of Achilles that Patroklos was wearing. Finally, the body of the fallen warrior may be desecrated or returned to the enemy according to the feelings of the victor.

Glossary

buckler a small, round shield held by a handle or worn on the arm. Buckler seems to be synonymous with any shield in the *Iliad*.

bronze alloy of copper and tin. Frequently used in metalworking and decoration at the time of the Trojan War. Bronze was often used as a symbol in Greek literature for the age of the Trojan War, i.e., the Bronze Age.

carrion birds any birds that scavenge on dead flesh (carrion) such as vultures or crows.

Cronus early god in Greek mythology. Son of Uranus and father of Zeus, Poseidon, Hades, Hera, and Demeter.

funeral pyre a pile, especially of wood, on which a dead body is burned in a funeral rite.

Book VIII

In Book VIII, the Achaian, Teucer, hides behind the shield of Aias and kills several Trojans with his arrows. This style of fighting is unusual in the *Iliad* and seems almost dishonorable compared to most of the fights. Ennis Rees, who did the original Modern Library translation of the *Iliad*, has called the description of Teucer's battle, "The little *aristeia* of Little Teucer," which is as good a description as any.

Teucer's method of fighting, with bow and arrow, is unusual in the *Iliad*. Pandaros and Meriones are also mentioned as archers. The use of archery was probably associated only with certain of the Achaian kingdoms, possibly Lycia. In the *Odyssey*, Odysseus strings his bow and proceeds to kill many of the suitors with arrows, so that archery may also have been practiced in Ithaca.

Many critics and commentators have mentioned the beautiful simile that ends Book VIII. In the simile the watch fires of the Achaian camp are compared to the stars. The simile ends with an image of the horses standing, waiting for dawn. The peacefulness of the simile contrasts with the barbarity of the fighting that has occurred in Books VII and VIII. The simile also suggests a kind of optimism for the Greeks. They have been sorely pressed by the Trojans in Book VIII, but the scene around the campfire suggests a kind of serenity that belies concerns about defeat.

Glossary

charioteer the driver of a chariot. The fighter was not responsible for driving, only for fighting.

driver another term for charioteer.

herald an official messenger, usually allowed to pass through enemy lines to deliver a message.

Ida central mountain in the Troad range. Favorite seat of Zeus. Ida is probably the second most frequently mentioned mountain in the *Iliad* after Olympos.

Tartarus lowest part of the Greek underworld where Zeus' defeated enemies were sent.

tripod three-legged iron pot, used for cooking.

Book IX

Summary

The routed Achaian army is completely demoralized. At an assembly of troops that night, even proud King Agamemnon bursts into tears. He says that the war is lost, and he suggests sailing home. His dejected soldiers receive this speech in silence, but Diomedes leaps to his feet, reminding the king of his responsibilities and reminding the troops of their heroic heritage. They can *all* return home, he says, but *he*, Diomedes, will remain alone, if necessary, to continue fighting, for it is fated that Troy *will eventually fall.* This brave declaration restores the confidence of the army and, on the recommendation of Nestor, guards are posted at the wall and the troops disperse to their tents for dinner and sleep.

At a meeting of the council, old Nestor takes the floor and reminds Agamemnon that the absence of Achilles is causing the present distress of the army. The king admits that he was unwise to have insulted the great warrior. He decides to offer many valuable gifts, as well as the return of Briseis, if Achilles will rejoin the army. Emissaries are therefore sent to the tent of the sulking hero with this message.

Achilles welcomes Telamonian Aias (Ajax) and Odysseus with great honor, but he refuses to accept the terms offered by Agamemnon. He cannot be bought or sold, he says, and nothing, even if it were all the wealth of Egypt, could erase Agamemnon's public insult. Therefore, he *will not* join in the battle, and in the morning, he and his men will sail for home. He is adamant in his decision.

Back in the Achaian camp, Agamemnon listens with great sorrow to the report of what happened in Achilles' tent. Finally, Diomedes rises and tells the assembled warriors that it was an error to try to appeal to someone as conceited and headstrong as Achilles. He advises them to make whatever preparations are possible to defend the ships against the Trojans the next morning. All agree, and after making libations to the gods, they retire to their quarters.

Commentary

More than one commentator has referred to Book IX as a short manual of oratory. The Greeks considered oratory as a skill on the same level as fighting ability. The long, taunting battle speeches are an integral part of what a warrior should know. Phoenix reminds Achilles of how important oratorical skill is, and Odysseus is as highly regarded for his speaking as Achilles is for his fighting.

Odysseus, the great orator, makes the initial plea to Achilles. His speech follows the form of classical oratory, though in a shortened form. He begins by complimenting Achilles and attempting to make the great warrior receptive to the argument. The classical rhetoricians called these opening remarks the *exordium*.

Next, Odysseus explains the serious military situation of the Achaians to Achilles. This explanation of the situation was known as the *narratio*. In presenting the situation, Odysseus presents the patriotic argument for Achilles' returning to the battle.

Odysseus follows the narratio with the *conformatio*, or proof for his case. His proof consists of the moral argument—that Achilles' father, Peleus, had told his son to control his temper—and the material argument—the many rewards that Agamemnon has offered. Odysseus wisely leaves out Agamemnon's arrogant statement that he is Achilles' superior.

Finally, Odysseus reaches his conclusion by returning to the patriotic argument. He tells Achilles that he can achieve personal honor and glory by saving the Achaians.

Theme

Achilles response is swift and at first does not seem well thought-out. This event is one of the major turning points in the story. Until now, it was possible to sympathize with Achilles because Agamemnon had clearly been in the wrong; but with Achilles' refusal to accept the honorable terms offered to him, he puts his *injured pride* above all other considerations, and the moral balance begins to fall against him. Nothing will satisfy Achilles now except the complete humbling of Agamemnon, an unreasonable and unwarranted demand. Achilles' desire for revenge has begun to overwhelm his better judgement, his loyalty to his friends, and the very code of chivalric honor that he claims to hold so dear. In fact, Achilles openly questions the validity of the entire heroic code of honor. Indeed, this is a defining moment for Achilles, as he is a man of great passion and is a true fighter. The irony is inescapable.

Some critics interpret this episode differently, however. They believe that Achilles' reasons for refusing the offer are psychologically and morally valid because he does not need the gifts that Agamemnon offers to him. He knows that he will die shortly after the reconciliation is effected; and most importantly, he knows that if Agamemnon took away a gift earlier on a whim (Achilles' war prize, Briseis), then nothing will stop him from doing the same thing again.

Whichever view is accepted, the death of Patroklos (Achilles' warrior-companion) follows directly from this incident, and whether ultimately right or wrong, Achilles has freely chosen *not to accept* an honorable settlement, and thus he is responsible for what follows—that is, the death of Patroklos.

The other speeches in Book IX also follow the patterns of Greek classical oratory. Odysseus presents the argument from reason. Phoenix follows with the moral argument. Finally, Aias concludes with the emotional argument. Only Aias has any discernible effect on Achilles.

Finally, in Nestor's speech to Agamemnon early in Book IX, the old soldier argues that while a King must make decisions, he also must listen to advice. Nestor's words are echoed a few hundred years later when Creon in Sophocles' *Antigone* says that a good King will heed advice, which he immediately fails to do and so is brought low. Further, Agamemnon's much-discussed lines, in which he says that his madness, or *até*, (also translated as "delusion" or "ruin") caused him to take Briseis from Achilles, is parallel to the reasoning of Hamlet in Act V when he apologizes to Laertes for killing Polonius. Hamlet says that his "madness" caused him to kill Polonius, thereby absolving himself of responsibility for his actions much the same way Agamemnon does.

Glossary

embassy a mission, especially one undertaken by an ambassador. The warriors in Book IX are symbolic ambassadors from Agamemnon to Achilles.

oratory oratory, the art of speaking, was one of the classical areas of learning for ancient Greeks. A classical oratory consisted of pre-scribed sections: *exordium, narratio,* and *conformatio.* (See the Commentary on Book IX for a discussion of these terms.)

Phoenix tutor and friend of Achilles.

Book X

Summary

Agamemnon is unable to sleep because of his concern about the fate of the Achaian army. After much tossing and turning, he rises and awakens all his senior commanders. Old Nestor advises that under cover of darkness a scout be sent into the Trojan camp. With luck, this maneuver will enable them to learn the strengths, as well as the plans, of the enemy.

Diomedes volunteers to reconnoiter behind the Trojan lines, and he selects Odysseus to accompany him. The two men arm themselves and set out. In the area between the camps, they capture Dolon, a Trojan nobleman who was sent by Hektor to conduct a reconnaissance of the Achaian camp. The warriors promise Dolon that they will not harm him and from him they learn the whereabouts of Hektor and his staff, key information about the various units of the Trojan army, and the precautions that the Trojans have taken to guard the camp. Diomedes then treacherously kills the Trojan spy. The two Achaian heroes also learn that a new contingent of troops from Thrace lies asleep and unprotected on the Trojan flank. They kill many of these warriors until Apollo intervenes.

After returning to camp the two warriors take a ritual bath.

Commentary

Book X, often called the *Doloneia*, provides a bridge between the speeches of Book IX and the extended battle scenes in Books XI–XVIII. Book X deals with a totally different aspect of war—espionage. The episode with Odysseus, Diomedes, and the Trojan, Dolon, contrasts with the straightforward battle scenes where carnage and brutality are paired with nobility and honor. The events in Book X are still violent, but there is no honor or nobility to offset the brutality. The foray of Diomedes and Odysseus is a foray behind enemy lines by men without scruples. Later in the Middle Ages, Dante noted this aspect of the passage and placed Diomedes and Odysseus in the 8th Circle of Hell, Bolgia, the Evil Counselors. The deceitful murder of Dolon is Dante's basis for this placement.

Literary Device

The bath that Diomedes and Odysseus take in the sea at the end of Book X may be symbolic of their need to cleanse themselves both physically and spiritually of this dirty night's work. The events in Book X, in fact, have often been referred to as "dirty work." That Homer looked on the deceitful killing of Dolon as low, immoral business is accentuated by the ironic ritual cleansing the two warriors go through after they have committed the murder of Dolon and the sleeping Trojans. Homer's consummate artistry shows up time and time again in the way the small events in the poem relate to larger issues.

At the end of Book X, Apollo, unable to put up with the slaughter of the sleeping Trojans, awakens Hippocoon, a Trojan captain. Earlier, Athena had helped Odysseus and Diomedes; now Apollo helps the Trojans. This recurring theme of the gods' involvement in human affairs continues to emphasize the anthropomorphic nature of the Greek gods and to show how the two groups—gods and men—deal with similar concerns on different levels. Behind this interference of the gods though, lies fate, which cannot be changed. Apollo cannot save Dolon, nor can he ultimately save the Trojans from losing the war. The gods have their own sympathies in the battle, but they also have certain limitations.

Glossary

brooch an ornament held by a pin or clasp and worn near the neck.

Doloneia name sometimes given to Book X for the Trojan character Dolon who is killed by Odysseus and Diomede.

tunic a loose, gownlike garment worn by men and women in ancient Greece and Rome.

Book XI

Summary

Agamemnon leads the Achaians into battle, and, at first, they prevail, driving the Trojans back as far as the city gates. But then, in quick succession, Agamemnon and most of the other Achaian leaders are wounded and are forced to withdraw from the fighting. The Trojans soon regain the ground they lost, and they inflict many casualties on the Achaians.

Clearly, Achilles has continued to observe the progress of the battle, and although he is unable to voice the feeling, he is obviously troubled by the dangerous predicament of his Achaian comrades-at-arms and by his own *self-imposed inability* to help them. But he senses with some relief that the time is drawing near when he will be able to get satisfaction for his wounded pride. Thus, he sends Patroklos to get information from old Nestor because his own pride will not allow him to show any interest in the fate of the Achaians.

In the Achaian camp, old Nestor gives Patroklos a long account of the day's events, with many reminiscences of past battles. Finally, coming to the point, he convinces Patroklos to try yet another time to persuade Achilles to return to battle against the Trojans. If Patroklos cannot do this, Nestor says, perhaps Patroklos himself could put on the armor of Achilles and join in the fighting. Nestor says that if the Trojans were to recognize the mighty Achilles' armor, they would think that Achilles had settled his dispute with Agamemnon and that he had returned to the battlefront. This strategy alone may be sufficient to save the day. Patroklos is impressed by this advice and returns to Achilles' tent.

Commentary

Character Insight

From Book I to Book IX, the anger of Achilles seems justified. But, Achilles' petulant refusal of Agamemnon's offer of atonement in Book IX sets up a reversal of positions. No longer does Achilles' wrath have a moral force behind it; now it seems childish and pointless. Earlier, Agamemnon had appeared weak and haughty, but in Book XI he emerges as a great warrior and leader. Book XI is, in fact, the *aristeia* of Agamemnon as he battles majestically across the field. In Book XI, Homer moves into the second of the great structural waves of the *Iliad*—Books IX–XVIII—where Achilles is clearly in the wrong and Agamemnon in the right.

Among several important battle incidents in Book XI is the wounding of Diomedes by Paris. Paris shoots an arrow that hits Diomedes in the foot. This incident shows Paris' prowess with the bow and foreshadows the death of Achilles. Paris eventually kills Achilles with an arrow shot into the Greek's vulnerable heel.

Nestor is once again presented in a humorous light in Book XI. He helps Machaon, the wounded surgeon from the field. Once they are out of danger, Nestor pulls up chairs for them and begins to reminisce about the old days. Around them the battle rages, but Nestor is intent on his stories. Like all garrulous old men, he recalls the older times and heroes as superior to the present. Nestor is, of course, more than a comic figure—his stories do tie in importantly with the action—but his attitude and actions are so stereotypical that the comic implications cannot be overlooked.

Finally, Book XI contains a major turning point in the *Iliad*. Achilles decides to send Patroklos to check on the wounded Machaon. This action by Achilles shows that he is following the battle with interest, but it also sets in motion the events that will lead to Achilles' re-entry into the battle. By letting Patroklos take his own place in checking on Machaon, Achilles foreshadows his allowing Patroklos to enter the battle—a step that will lead to the death of Patroklos.

Theme

Book XI also refers to the Greek belief concerning burial of the dead. After Odysseus kills Socus, he taunts the body: "Now your father and noble mother/ will never close your eyes in death—screaming vultures/ will claw them out of you, wings beating your corpse!" The Greeks believed that if a body was not buried, the soul would wander eternally seeking rest. This belief is described in Sophocles' *Antigone*, as well, where Creon refuses to bury the body of Oedipus' son Polynices. Homer, in the *Iliad*, accentuates the horror of war by having Odysseus do more than kill Socus; he condemns him to an eternity of pain and sorrow. This idea will come up again at the end of the poem when Achilles does even worse to the body of Hektor.

At the end of Book XI appears a reference to the centaur, Cheiron. In mythology, Cheiron was a wise centaur who taught Achilles. In the *Inferno* of Dante's Divine Comedy, Dante assigns Cheiron as one of the guards of the Violent Against Neighbor in the River of Blood. Oddly, Dante does not place Achilles in the River of Blood but places him with the Lustful in Circle II because of his love for Polyxena, Priam's daughter.

Glossary

bastard not a pejorative term for an illegitimate child but more of a description. Bastard children were acknowledged and honored, although they were not considered royalty.

lion lions and other large beasts of prey were common in ancient Greece and Asia Minor.

triple-flanged a flange is a ridge used for guiding a projectile. The Greek arrows have three edges or flanges.

Books XII to XV

Summary

Books XII to XV

The Achaians are forced to take refuge behind their wall while the Trojans continue their brutal assault. But the Trojans soon discover that they are unable to cross the Achaian trench in their chariots, so they attack on foot. Much bloody combat ensues.

Then suddenly an eagle with a serpent in its talons flies over the Trojan army; Poulydamas, a Trojan commander, interprets this as a bad omen and asks Hektor to fall back, but the commander refuses. The attack continues and after several attempts, the Achaian wall is broken. Forcing open one of the gates with a large stone, Hektor and his men storm inside. The Achaians retreat in panic and take refuge among their ships.

Zeus has brought Hektor and the Trojans as far as the Achaian ships, so now he relaxes and turns his attention to other matters. Poseidon takes advantage of Zeus' lapse of attention to come to the aid of the Achaians and, disguised as Kalchas, he moves among the Achaian ranks, encouraging them to continue fighting.

While the violent battle continues, old Nestor seeks out Agamemnon, Diomedes, and Odysseus, all three of whom are wounded. Nestor wants to devise a plan of action. Agamemnon is certain that the defeat of the Achaian army has been willed by heaven, and he can think only of having the troops retreat and board their ships, escaping by sea. Odysseus points out that this is not only dishonorable but that it would be extremely dangerous. It would be very difficult, he says, to launch and board their ships while under attack. To do this may make a Trojan victory even easier. The leaders then decide to go among the ranks and encourage their men.

From Olympos, Hera notices how Poseidon, the sea god, is trying to aid the Achaians, and so she makes plans to occupy Zeus so that Poseidon will have even more opportunity to help the besieged

Achaians. Dressing in her finest garments and borrowing the magic girdle of Aphrodite, Hera flies off to Mount Ida, where Zeus is sitting. Her husband is overwhelmed by her charms, and Hera finds it easy to seduce him. As prearranged, the God of Sleep casts a spell over Zeus.

Commentary

Book XII

Book XII, sometimes called "the book of the wall," completes the first grand sweep of Trojan successes as Homer builds up to the re-entry of Achilles. The Book opens with the explanation that in the future the wall will be completely destroyed by Poseidon, showing the impermanence of human creation. The passage on the future of the wall is somewhat reminiscent of Shelley's "Ozymandias" that points out the futility of human pride. In both works, the impermanence of human accomplishments is contrasted with the overwhelming natural power of the universe.

Glossary

boundary stones boulders used to mark property lines in Greek communities.

casque a helmet; In anatomy the casque refers to a helmet-like body part; Homer, often refers to the skull with this term.

Cebriones one of Priam's bastard sons, killed by Achilles.

Polydamous one of the Trojan commanders.

Book XIII

Poseidon, having been introduced in Book XII, takes an even greater role in Book XIII. Book XIII is sometimes referred to as the *Poseidonead*. Poseidon rouses the Achaians to battle with *hortatory* speeches. These exhortations early in Book XIII are another typical facet of epic battle and once again accentuate the importance of oratory in Greek culture. Just as the speeches in Book IX reveal the oratorical skills of the warriors, so now in Book XIII the god is shown as a great orator as well as fighter.

In the last part of the book, old Idomeneus emerges as the principal fighter. The battle scenes in this book grow more intense as the fighting seems to move toward some climax. Idomeneus, the Cretan king, has his *aristeia* as he holds off the Trojan attackers.

Glossary

battalion   a large group of soldiers arrayed for battle.

bossed shield   decorated with raised ornaments. The more modern term would be *embossed*.

God of the Earthquake   Poseidon.

Panic   god who personifies fear and riot among the troops.

Book XIV

Book XIV continues the great battle near the Achaian ships but adds a new element—the tricking of Zeus. Several commentators have suggested that this book prefigures later mock epics such as *The Rape of the Lock*. Unquestionably, Homer here introduces a comic element as a break from the intense battle scenes that precede and follow the interlude between Hera and Zeus. The seduction of Zeus by Hera requires careful planning because she, in a very real sense, is subverting the will of the Father God in attempting to allow Poseidon to attack the Trojans unchecked.

The sash that Aphrodite gives Hera is of some interest. It has both sexually provocative pictures and words, one of the few references in the *Iliad* to writing.

Zeus' seduction speech to Hera must be one of the most unusual in the history of love and sex. Zeus essentially woos his wife with a report on his sexual conquests—an interesting tactic.

After Hera seduces Zeus and lulls him to sleep, the story returns to the battle, where, oddly, the Greek warriors exchange armor. This event has been frequently commented on, some suggesting that it shows a commingling of identities among the Achaian warriors, others finding it incomprehensible if not downright bizarre. Because the passage says, "The best men donned the best, the worst the worst," it seems that the idea is that for the upcoming charge, the greatest warriors need the best armor. To suggest that this is somehow a commingling of identity seems unlikely because the action is clearly to stratify the soldiers rather than bring them together.

At the end, Poseidon leads the Achaians into battle, perhaps symbolically showing that the Achaians literally have the sea at their backs.

Glossary

Sleep god who is the brother of Death.

Zeus' conquests Danae, Ixion's wife, Europa, Semele, Alcmena, Demeter, and Leto are all listed by Zeus as sexual conquests. This list is his strange means of seducing his wife, Hera.

Book XV

The second great surge forward by the Trojans occurs in Book XV. Zeus, having awakened to the Achaian rally, asserts his leadership, and no god dares stand in his way. Zeus stands in direct contrast with Agamemnon, whose leadership is frequently questioned and sometimes challenged.

Zeus presents the outcome of the battle. This passage is of interest because it points to the fact that Homer's audience was completely aware of the plot events of the poem. Homer does not have to depend on his plot to create interest. His audience is involved as they watch the inexorable tide of events surging toward their inevitable close. As with so many Greek works, the power lies in how the author handles his material as opposed to simply what happens.

Achilles' friend, Patroklos, who has been introduced earlier in the epic, becomes a major player in this book. Patroklos tries to persuade Achilles to enter the battle. Having failed in that attempt, Patroklos gets permission to enter himself. The discussion between Achilles and Patroklos shows that Achilles is in conflict regarding his position. He obviously wishes to return to battle, but cannot because of his vow and his pride. Oddly, Achilles seems more and more like a modern, alienated anti-hero—the man apart from everyone else, unable to act until action is forced upon him.

Apollo rouses Hektor to return to the battle. Once again the gods act as inspiration for the mortals. Symbolically, the God of War acts as the elemental force that drives men into battle. Consequently, Hektor, who had pulled back from the fight, finds renewed energy and surges forward.

Glossary

Styx, River of the Underworld Achilles was dipped in it by Thetis, making him invulnerable except for his heel. Gods also swore oaths by the River Styx.

Book XVI

Summary

While the battle around the ships continues, Patroklos pleads with Achilles to be allowed to wear Achilles' armor and to lead the Myrmidons, his troops, into battle. While Achilles is considering this request, flames are seen rising from among the ships, indicating great success for the Trojans. Achilles consents, and Patroklos and the Myrmidons arm themselves with great enthusiasm. After Achilles has addressed them and offered a libation to Zeus, he warns Patroklos to *do no more than rescue the ships*, for if he attacks Troy, he may be killed.

The Trojans are panicked by the belief that Achilles has decided to unleash his fury against them, and in a short time, the addition of Achilles' fresh and well equipped regiment of Myrmidons to the Achaian army destroys the Trojan advantage. Hektor and his men flee toward Troy.

Patroklos pursues Hektor and his men all the way to the walls of Troy, doing many heroic deeds on the way. However, Apollo decides to enter the fighting as an ally of Hektor, and while Patroklos, in an almost god-like manner, slaughters nine Trojans in a single charge, Apollo slips up behind him and strikes him so fiercely on the back that Patroklos' vizored helmet flies off. His spear is shattered and his armor falls to the ground. Then, while Patroklos is standing in a daze, a Trojan soldier pierces him midway between the shoulders with a javelin.

Patroklos tries to hide, but Hektor sees him and rams a spear through the lower part of his belly. Patroklos falls with a thud, and the entire Achaian army is stunned. His voice failing, Patroklos tells Hektor that it was not he who conquered him. It was the gods, he says, the gods and "deadly Destiny."

Commentary

This episode is the second turning point in the tragic story of Achilles. He has made a fatal decision, and the deaths of Sarpedon, Patroklos, Hektor, Achilles himself, and the fall of Troy all inevitably follow. The deaths of Sarpedon and Patroklos in this book introduce an elegiac tone into the last part of the *Iliad*, as the characters that the reader sees as sympathetic are killed. Until now, Achilles has been torn by a conflict between the noble elements of his soul, which urge him to help his Achaian friends, and his obsessive sense of honor, which demands the *full humiliation* of Agamemnon and a complete recognition of Achilles' own worth by the other Achaian warriors.

Character Insight

Achilles sees the disguise scheme suggested by Patroklos as the perfect solution to his dilemma: It would allow him to save his own ships and thus *fulfill his moral obligation* to the Achaians. Yet at the same time, he can *protect his prestige* because he himself would not have to intervene. This equivocating solution is the cause of all the tragic events to come. Achilles tries to rationalize his consent to the plan by claiming that he had sworn not to participate in the fighting unless his own ships were threatened; but in fact, he never really said this. What has happened is that Achilles is beginning to lose his ability to think clearly and weigh all the factors in this situation.

Achilles' horses, Roan Beauty and Dapple, are introduced, emphasizing the importance of horses in ancient warfare. As with human characters, the lineage of the horses is given.

Achilles takes his wine cup (kalyx) to make a special prayer to Zeus. Like his shield and spear, the wine cup is an object that only Achilles uses. Achilles' prayer is for Patroklos, and the reader immediately finds that Zeus will grant Patroklos success but denies him "safe and sound return from battle." Later, Zeus considers overturning fate to let his own son, Sarpedon, live. Hera overrules him, saying, "Do as you please, Zeus . . . / but none of the deathless gods will ever praise you." The clear suggestion is that Zeus has some control over fate; but like humans, he must generally accept the fate that has been decreed, for worse consequences occur when fate is tampered with.

Glossary

Glaucus Trojan ally who commands the Lycians.

intractable not tractable; specifically, *a*) hard to manage; unruly or stubborn *b*) hard to work, manipulate, cure, or treat; often used in describing Achilles.

Myrmidons soldiers commanded by Achilles.

Sarpedon Trojan ally, co-commander of the Lycians, killed by Patroklos. He was a son of Zeus.

Selli prophets who serve Zeus.

Book XVII

Summary

Menelaos attempts to protect the body of Patroklos from the enemy, but finally he is driven off by Hektor. The Trojan commander strips Achilles' beautiful armor from the corpse and puts it on in place of his own. Then almost immediately, a battle develops over Patroklos' naked corpse. The Trojans hope to take it to Troy to mutilate it as a warning to all the Achaians, and the Achaians want to give it a proper funeral ceremony. The leading warriors on both sides engage in this fight, and two gods, Apollo and Athena, also join. While this is going on, Hektor attempts to capture Achilles' horses, but they escape back to the Achaian camp. Finally, the body of Patroklos is rescued and is safely carried back to the Achaian camp.

Commentary

Book XVII at last gives the reader the *aristeia* of Menelaos. The capture of Menelaos' wife caused the Trojan War, yet he has for the most part been a bit player in the story, often looked out for by his older brother, Agamemnon. In Book XVII, he comes into his own as a warrior. However, even here Homer continues to use similes that seem to diminish Menelaos. In line 5 he is compared to a cow protecting its calf and later in this book he is compared to a fly. Menelaos is generally presented as a sympathetic character, but at the same time, this presentation often makes him seem somewhat less than many of the other Greek heroes.

The horses of Achilles weep for the dead Patroklos. This scene underscores the earlier introduction of these horses. This allows Homer to emphasize the point that even nature weeps for the dead Patroklos.

While most of Book XVII is battle description, the decision by Hektor to wear Achilles' armor is very suggestive. Hektor, the greatest of the Trojan warriors, seems by this act to associate himself as the equal of Achilles. Later events will show that Hektor's actions here are examples of *hubris*—sinful pride. In this book, Hektor and Aeneas sweep forward again, but their successes mark the beginning of the end in the *Iliad* for Trojan victories.

In lines 351–353, Aias dodges a spear that strikes and kills Schedius. This fortuitous dodging followed by an infortuitous death happens several times in the *Iliad* and becomes something of a cliché.

The Homeric Greeks believed that one's soul could not enter the afterworld unless *the proper burial rites* had been carried out—in this case, cremation and burial of the ashes under a barrow. The battle that takes place over the body of Patroklos is due to this belief.

Glossary

pathetic fallacy in literature, the attribution of human feelings and characteristics to inanimate things (for example, the angry sea, a stubborn door). While the weeping horses of Achilles could be called personification, they are more precisely examples of pathetic fallacy.

Son of Cronus epithet for Zeus. Cronus the Titan was Zeus' father.

yoke pads part of the accoutrements for harnessed oxen. The yoke pads kept the yokes from digging into the animal's skin.

Book XVIII

Summary

When Achilles learns of the death of Patroklos, he bursts into tears, tearing his hair and throwing himself on the ground. His sorrowful lament is heard by his mother, Thetis, and she comes to comfort him. She points out that if Achilles avenges Patroklos, he himself will be killed. Despite his mother's warning, however, Achilles chooses to undertake this risk, so great is his love for Patroklos. Thetis therefore promises to procure new armor for her son from the god Hephaistos to replace the armor that was captured by Hektor.

Meanwhile, the Achaians, who are bearing away the body of Patroklos, are given close pursuit by the Trojans; so Achilles (at the suggestion of Hera) appears at the Achaian trench and shouts his ferocious and furious war cry. The sound of this mighty war cry strikes terror into the hearts of the Trojans, and they retreat in panic.

Achilles' sorrow is intensified by the sight of his dead comrade's body, and all of the Achaians join Achilles in mourning. Achilles vows to kill Hektor and to slaughter twelve Trojan warriors on the funeral pyre of Patroklos. Meanwhile, Patroklos' dead body is washed clean and laid out in state in Achilles' tent.

At a Trojan council of war that night, Poulydamas suggests that the Trojan army remain in the city and fight off any Achaian assault from the protection of the battlements. The return of Achilles to the Achaian force makes it too dangerous to fight in the open, he says. Hektor refuses to heed this advice, however, and he insists that the Trojan army stay in the field. His opinion prevails.

On Olympos, Thetis calls upon Hephaistos. She tells the god about all that has taken place on the battlefield that day, and she asks him to provide new armor for her son. Hephaistos assents and makes a marvelous and beautiful set of new armor for Achilles. The new shield alone is a masterpiece, being built up of five layers and having on it a representation of the signs of the zodiac and of two cities engaged in all the peaceful and warlike activities of mankind. When the armor is finished, Thetis takes it in her arms, and, thanking Hephaistos, she goes to find her son.

Readers see, then, that Achilles is given his final chance to decide his fate, for Thetis tells him that he will die if he avenges Patroklos. Despite this knowledge, Achilles chooses to continue his plan for revenge. Patroklos was his closest friend, a lesser reflection of his own glory, and, in an emotional sense, part of himself; so in every way, the killing of Patroklos was a direct blow to Achilles himself. His determination to avenge his friend is so intense because he realizes that he is responsible for Patroklos' death, and he is angry with himself as well as with the Trojans. He hopes that by punishing the Trojans and, in particular, by venting his fury on Hektor, their leader and the human symbol of Trojan resistance, he will be able to assuage his sense of guilt and grief.

In all things, Achilles has a greater capacity for feeling than other men do. His wrath, his grief, and his exploits in the battle to come will now begin to take on a superhuman quality, symbolized in part by the divine armor made for him by the god Hephaistos, as the climax of the tragedy draws near.

Commentary

Book XVIII is made up of three major parts. First, after Achilles breaks down at the news of Patroklos' death, Thetis comes to comfort her son. Much of this scene is a foreshadowing of the later death of Achilles. Second, in a long middle section, Achilles goes to the trench and recovers the body of Patroklos. Third, and finally, the new shield is created.

Literary Device

A number of commentators have suggested that the first part of Book XVIII is drawn from descriptions of the death of Achilles. Achilles pours ashes on Patroklos' face and body. Weeping Nereids appear around him like mourners at a funeral. Thetis, standing, cradles his head like a mother holding a dead son lying on a bier, as Kakridis notes. The entire scene seems drawn from, and simultaneously points to, the eventual death of Achilles.

A further fatalistic element in the scene is Achilles' statement, "I've lost the will to live," along with the overriding fact that he will be killed if he returns to the battle. Of course, Achilles also ends his first wrath here and anticipates reconciliation with Agamemnon. Conversely, Achilles also initiates his second wrath at this point. This second wrath does not end until he reaches reconciliation with Priam.

In the middle section of Book XVIII, Achilles goes forth to help recover Patroklos' body. His war cry, announcing his presence, strikes terror in the Trojans. In their hurried council, the Trojans make the mistake of following the advice of Hektor rather than of Poulydamus. Poulydamas was born on the same night as Hektor and symbolically serves as his alter ego. Just as Achilles, through his actions, moves toward his own death, so Hektor, through his mistakes, moves toward his. There is a sense of dreadful irony hanging over these two scenes and characters.

The last section of Book XVIII describes the giant shield that Hephaistos, God of the Forge, made for Achilles. The description of the shield is a digression justified by the fact that Hektor now has Achilles' armor. Homer structured the *Iliad* so that at any point he could discuss any subject he chose. The description of the shield allows Homer to depict the world. Each circle on the shield shows some aspect of the classical world that Homer knew or imagined. It is, in a sense, what the war is about.

Glossary

black ashes the black ashes in this book are symbolic of death and mourning.

Nereids daughters of the sea-god, Nereus.

Old Man of the Sea Nereus, father of Thetis and the Nereids.

Book XIX

Summary

After receiving his new armor, Achilles calls for an assembly of the Achaian army. Then he announces that his quarrel with King Agamemnon is ended and that he is ready to return to war. This speech is applauded with great joy by all the troops. Agamemnon rises and welcomes Achilles back to the army. He says that at the time of their disagreement, he had been blinded and robbed of his wits by Zeus. He states that in compensation to Achilles, he will return Briseis to him, as well as shower upon him many other presents.

Achilles accepts the offer, but clearly he is more eager to attack the Trojans than he is to collect gifts. He demands that the army go into action at once. Odysseus sympathizes with Achilles' zeal, but he points out that the troops are tired and hungry and that they need some time to renew themselves before fighting again. Achilles agrees to wait. He announces that the troops may eat if they wish, but he himself is going to fast until Patroklos is avenged.

When the Achaian troops are once more ready to fight, Achilles puts on his splendid new armor, and then, mounting his chariot, he prepares to lead the army. But first, he reproaches his horses for allowing Patroklos to be killed. One of the horses answers, saying that Patroklos' death was not their fault, but that it was caused by Apollo and Destiny. The horse then prophesies the eventual death of Achilles on the battlefield. Achilles answers that he already knows about his doom, but that nothing will prevent him from avenging Patroklos. With this, Achilles shouts his mighty war cry and gallops into battle.

Throughout the *Iliad*, Achilles has been a creature of extremes—a man of absolute feelings and absolute reactions. Now that he is finally reconciled with Agamemnon, his passion to avenge Patroklos becomes as intense and impatient as was his former, selfish desire for the satisfaction of his honor. No longer concerned with such human "trivialities" as eating or resting, Achilles is transformed into a kind of cosmic figure, an archetypal hero sweeping through all opposition, divine and human, to achieve his ends.

Commentary

The reconciliation that ends the first wrath of Achilles and the actions that initiate the second both occur in Book XIX. The book is made up of two main sections: the reconciliation between Agamemnon and Achilles, and Achilles' preparation for battle.

The reconciliation between Agamemnon and Achilles brings closure to the incident that began the *Iliad*. In a sense, Achilles rejoins the ranks of the Achaians, and Agamemnon once again becomes the undisputed leader of the Greek forces. That Agamemnon has difficulty apologizing to Achilles is obvious from his attitude, speech, and ideas. For example, he never calls Achilles directly by name, and he tries to avoid taking responsibility for his actions. He essentially says, "The devil made me do it," as an explanation for his decision to take Briseis. The actual word Agamemnon uses is not "devil" but *até* (*Ruin* in the Fagles translation). *Até* is often translated as "delusion" rather than "ruin" and was a Greek all-purpose excuse for irrational acts. Moreover, blaming one's actions on an outside force is similar to the recurring image in the *Iliad* of gods speaking directly to humans to influence their actions. This idea adds some substantiation to the psychological notion that the gods, in this case *até*, represent a part of the human mind. Therefore Agamemnon is perhaps blaming his irrationality on a voice that led him astray.

One other interesting facet of the Greek council of reconciliation is the mild dispute between Odysseus and Achilles over food. Achilles rejects the suggestion that the Greeks should feast before the battle. He says, "I have no taste for food." Odysseus responds with the very practical idea that an army must have nourishment to fight. In history, battles have frequently been decided in favor of the side that was properly fed and therefore able to be sustained on the field. In terms of characters in the *Iliad*, Odysseus is the logical one to appreciate the idea that soldiers need to eat and refresh themselves before battle. Some commentators have questioned the dramatic purpose of this conversation and the delay in the narrative that it produces. Nonetheless, the discussion points out the distinction between the wrathful warrior, Achilles, and the practical tactician, Odysseus. Eventually, Achilles dies in battle while Odysseus makes his long but successful journey home.

In the next section of Book XIX, Achilles arms for battle. As Achilles puts on his armor, Homer describes the scene with images that accentuate the idea of loneliness. The shine on the armor is compared to the light of the moon at sea or a watchfire at a sheepfold on a mountain slope. Achilles, even in reconciliation, is a man apart from others.

Literary Device

Finally, as Achilles prepares his horses and chariot for battle, his horse, Roan Beauty, responds to the warrior's encouragement by reminding its master that Achilles will soon die in battle himself. The horse's speech is totally unexpected and one of the few supernatural moments in the poem, aside from the frequent interventions of the gods. Some commentators analyze this passage as Achilles talking to himself. The speech of the horses foreshadows the impending death of Achilles and intensifies his own fatalistic feelings. The fact that Homer uses the horses for the purpose of foreshadowing allows Homer to step outside the narrative momentarily and make what is almost an authorial comment on the significance of Achilles' decision to fight. The horse's speech is followed by the war cry of Achilles and the second wrath begins.

Glossary

ambrosia the food of the gods.

Furies avenging spirits, often used as symbols of a destructive, guilty conscience, especially in matters involving wrongs within a family. The Furies typically exacted vengeance when no human agent was available to do so.

Ruin (Ate) Ruin or Ate is a personified goddess who represents "delusion" or "madness" and the destruction that can result. Ruin is used by Agamemnon to explain his inexplicable actions toward Achilles.

tactician epithet frequently used with Odysseus to emphasize his intellectual and practical abilities.

Book XX

Summary

While the Achaian and Trojan armies group for battle, Zeus calls for an assembly of all the gods. When they have gathered, he gives them permission to openly assist either of the factions, for Achilles must be prevented from overstepping the bounds that fate has set on his achievements. At once, Hera, Athena, Poseidon, Hermes, and Hephaistos leave to join the Achaians, while Ares, Apollo, Artemis, and Aphrodite fly to the side of the Trojans.

The battle opens with great fury. Achilles is about to kill Aeneas when Poseidon rescues the Trojan prince. Poseidon does so because Aeneas has been fated to be the sole survivor of the house of Priam. But, undaunted by divine interference of Poseidon, Achilles continues fighting, slaughtering many of the Trojans and sweeping through the field unchecked. Many Trojans die at his hands.

Commentary

Book XX serves as an interlude before the *aristeia* of Achilles in Books XXI and XXII, which culminates in the death of Hektor. The council of the gods at the start of Book XX sets up the fighting (*theomachy*) between the pro-Greek and pro-Trojan deities that continue into Book XXI.

A much commented-on section of Book XX deals with Aeneas. Aeneas' fame today, of course, comes from Virgil's great epic, *The Aeneid*, which was modeled on Homer's works. Aeneas is introduced early on in the *Iliad*, but up until Book XX he plays only a minor role. In this book, his prominence serves only as a dramatic diversion whereby Homer delays the fight between Hector and Achilles.

At line 345, Poseidon prophesies that Aeneas will survive the battle. Ironically, because of Virgil, Poseidon's prophecy is true in a much greater way than Homer could possibly have intended: The Trojan survivor becomes one of the great epic heroes of world literature. One theory exists that the section on Aeneas was added to the *Iliad* to honor a Greek family that claimed descent from Aeneas. Whatever the validity of that idea, the Roman Empire eventually claimed Aeneas as its founder, through the Julian line. From that tradition, Virgil chose to create his epic character.

The *aristeia* of Achilles begins in the last part of Book XX and continues in the next two books.

Glossary

theomachy a battle of the gods, frequently used in mythological traditions.

threshing floor floor or platform where seed was separated from a plant by striking the plant against the hard surface.

Book XXI

Summary

The Trojan troops flee in terror from Achilles. One portion of the army heads for the city while another group seeks refuge near the River Xanthos. Achilles cuts off the second group and kills many of them as they try to cross the stream. He also takes twelve captives, as he vowed he would. The slaughter continues, and soon the river is choked with bodies.

The god of the river is antagonized by all this bloodshed in his waters, and so he attacks Achilles with great waves and currents. Achilles begins to falter under this onslaught, but Poseidon and Athena reassure him, while Hera and Hephaistos attack the river with fire. Seeing his water boil away in great, mysterious heat, Xanthos relents.

Following this, the gods also engage in combat, so excited are they by human warfare. Athena defeats Ares and Aphrodite, while Hera drives Artemis from the field. Poseidon challenges Apollo, but the younger god does not accept his uncle's dare because of deference to his age.

Achilles continues to chase the Trojans, and Agenor, a half-brother of Hektor, attempts to fight him in single combat; but Agenor is far inferior to Achilles, and Apollo finally rescues him. This diversion allows most of the retreating troops enough time to take refuge in the city.

Commentary

In the first section of Book XXI, Achilles kills Lykaon, a son of Priam. The unimportant Lykaon is used as a stand-in for all the lesser characters who have been and will be killed by the heroes of the *Iliad*. The attention given to Lykaon—his history and the account of his death—makes the incident stand out in the poem. The most poignant moment comes when Achilles rejects Lykaon's plea for his life, saying, "Come friend, you too must die." Achilles follows this remark with a reminder of Patroklos' death and with the prediction of his own death. He establishes a kinship with Lykaon, assuring the doomed Trojan that all men must face the moment of death. Achilles' attitude is much like that of Hamlet—"Readiness is all." The killing of Lykaon is a *fait accompli*, and Achilles performs the deed almost as a duty, fully aware of the imminence of his own death in battle.

A slightly ironic commentary on Achilles eventual death occurs in his battle with the river. The river, rising in flood against Achilles because of all the dead bodies thrown in it, sweeps Achilles away. Achilles, who is often an overpowering natural force against the Trojans, is here thwarted and almost killed by the natural force of the river. Achilles is so alarmed by the river that he becomes fearful of ignominious death by drowning rather than the glorious death in battle that has been prophesied. Only the intervention of Hera through Hephaistos, as God of Fire, saves Achilles. Symbolically, the two great elemental forces of fire and water are in conflict, with Achilles in the middle.

Literary Device

This dramatic scene with the river begins the *theomachy*, or battle of the gods. The theomachy produces a lowering both of tone and intensity in the epic. Zeus laughs "deep in his own great heart, delighted/ to see the gods engage in all out combat." Briefly, Achilles is ignored as the central focus of the scene shifts from humanity's life and death struggle to the play-like warfare of the gods. The battle of the gods has received much criticism over the years. Many commentators think that the theomachy lowers the tone of the poem just as it builds toward its climactic moments. The fight among the gods borders on slapstick comedy and adds little to the developing rage of Achilles. The general defense of the theomachy has been that it serves as a type of comic relief allowing the tension that the reader has developed concerning Achilles to lessen before the confrontation with Hektor. It is also quite probable that Homer's original audience (and others since) simply enjoyed the spectacle of a fight among gods.

Book XXI concludes with Achilles' encounter with Agenor. Agenor is simply one more dramatic obstacle that Homer creates to delay the confrontation between Hector and Achilles. Agenor does have a soliloquy, one of four such speeches in the *Iliad*. The others are by Odysseus, Menelaos, and Hektor. Of these, Agenor's is the most unusual, because it is by a minor character. In his speech, Agenor seems to anticipate the scene between Hektor and Achilles in the next book, and his speech is, therefore, a type of foreshadowing.

Glossary

Agenor Trojan warrior, one of Antenor's sons. Saved from Achilles by Apollo.

hospitality the tradition of hospitality demanded that even enemies provide protection for guests and hosts. This tradition carries on into the nineteenth and even twentieth centuries.

locusts any of various large grasshoppers; specifically, a migratory grasshopper often traveling in great swarms and destroying nearly all vegetation in areas visited.

Lykaon son of Priam though not of Hekuba. He is killed by Achilles in a poignant scene.

Xanthus another name for the River Scamander.

Book XXII

Summary

With the Trojans now secure in their city, Hektor—as their sole representative—stands outside the city gates and prepares to meet Achilles. His mother and father appeal to him to seek safety behind the city walls, but their pleas are in vain. While waiting, Hektor considers the various courses of action open to him and decides that the only real possibility is to fight Achilles.

Yet, when Achilles arrives, Hektor is overcome by fear and he flees. Achilles pursues him around the city walls three times, and, as they run, Hektor tries unsuccessfully to draw Achilles within range of the Trojan archers on the battlements.

Finally, Athena deludes Hektor into believing that he will have assistance against Achilles. He turns and stands his ground. But before the two heroes fight, Hektor attempts to make Achilles promise to treat his body with respect if he is killed, but Achilles is so full of fury that he refuses.

The two warriors engage in a decisive duel. Achilles casts his spear first and misses the mark, but it is returned to him by Athena. Next, Hektor throws his spear and hits the center of Achilles' shield, but the divine armor cannot be penetrated. The two men circle each other, slowly closing in. Hektor is armed with only a sword, while Achilles still has his spear. After several feints, Achilles lunges and stabs Hektor in the throat. As the Trojan dies, he begs that his body be returned to his family for a proper funeral, but Achilles again refuses Hektor's request. Hektor dies reminding Achilles that his own death is imminent.

All the Achaians run up to see the corpse of the almost-mythic, now-dead Trojan leader. Many of them jest and stab Hektor's corpse. Achilles strips off Hektor's armor and fastens his naked body to his chariot by the heels. Then he gallops off, dragging the corpse behind him in disgrace.

When Priam and Hekuba, Hektor's parents, witness the vicious treatment of their dead son, they begin to wail and bemoan their fate, and all of the citizens of Troy join in the piteous lamentations. The sound of this weeping is heard by Andromache, and when she learns of her husband's death, she collapses.

Commentary

Structurally, this book has three early appeals to Hektor, begging him to come inside the walls of Troy, balanced late in the book by three laments for Hektor's death. In between occurs the fight between Hektor and Achilles.

Theme

The battle between Hektor and Achilles brings about a reconsideration of two ideas that have been implicit throughout the *Iliad*. The first idea is the conflict between the values symbolized by the two warriors. The second idea is the nature of the relationship between the gods and men.

The duel between Hektor and Achilles has been interpreted as a clash between two diametrically opposed world views: Hektor, the representative of hearth, home, and city-state, is the defender of the principles of individual self-control and of a constructive, positive way of life. Achilles is the personification of primitive brutality, anti-social destructiveness, and undisciplined instinct. Thus, it is a fight where human civilization itself is at stake, and although the destructive forces triumph, Achilles (their embodiment) is rehabilitated and rejuvenated in the final book of the epic. The institutions represented by Hektor are reborn in a new form during the confrontation between Achilles and Hektor's aged father, Priam.

Two scenes explore the god/human relationship in complementary fashion. Zeus considers saving Hektor's life by "plucking the man from death." Athena counters that Zeus can do as he pleases, "but none of the deathless gods will ever praise you."

The first suggestion in this scene is that Zeus can overcome fate, but only in a way that brings turmoil to heaven and earth. The second suggestion is that Zeus' intervention in human affairs in this instance is not justifiable because fate has decreed otherwise. Hektor is preordained to die at the hands of Achilles, so there is no justification for intervention.

This second idea about the nature of the relationships between gods and men is reinforced in the much discussed role of Athena in Hektor's death. Hektor runs when he first encounters Achilles, and the pall mall race around the walls of Troy is almost humorous. However, this race has to end and the inevitable conflict must take place. Athena intervenes in the form of Deiphobus and convinces Hektor to fight. Hektor does so and dies.

Commentary has focused on Athena's role, suggesting that Homer shows the gods as tricksters who cannot be trusted by humans. Actually, the opposite view is more accurate. Athena intervenes on the side of what *must* happen. Unlike Zeus' notion to save Hektor and avoid fate, Athena's goal is precisely to bring about what fate has decreed. She does not cause Hektor's death; instead she ends his unseemly flight and makes him turn to face what must be. Here again, the voice of the god is like the voice in the mind telling the hero what he must do. A heroic warrior cannot run from his foe, even if that foe is the invulnerable and deadly Achilles. The gods sometimes help humans face up to their human obligations and destinies.

For Achilles, the nature of his society and values, where competition and victory are everything, leaves him alone at the end of the battle, waiting for his own certain death.

Glossary

Deiphobus son of Priam, brother of Hektor; wisely advises Hektor to return within the walls of Troy.

Orion's Dog the Dog Star, Sirius, named for the dog of the mythological hunter, Orion.

Book XXIII

Summary

After returning to the Achaian camp, Achilles and the Myrmidons drive their chariots in a ritual procession around the bier of Patroklos, and Achilles leads his men in a dirge for the dead hero. That night, a funeral feast is held. Afterward, while he sleeps, Achilles has a vision of the ghost of Patroklos in which his friend asks that his funeral be held so that he can enter the realm of the dead in peace.

In the morning, the soldiers fetch wood and build a large funeral pyre. The army marches out in full military regalia, and the body of Patroklos is placed on top of the pyre. Several horses and hunting dogs, as well as the twelve captive Trojan noblemen, are sacrificed on the lower part of the accumulation of wood. The whole pile is then set on fire. After the flames have burned for a while, the fire is extinguished with wine, and the bones of Patroklos are placed in a jar for future burial alongside the body of Achilles. A memorial barrow is erected over the remains of the funeral pyre.

Achilles now proclaims that funeral games will be held in honor of his friend. Contests in chariot racing, boxing, wrestling, running, dueling, discus throwing, archery, and javelin throwing ensue, and valuable prizes are awarded.

During this time, the body of Hektor lies on the ground untended, but Apollo and Aphrodite protect the corpse from the ravages of stray dogs and the heat.

Commentary

Beginning in Book XXII and extending to Book XXIV, Achilles again moves from understandable anger, this time over the death of Patroklos, to uncontrollable and all-consuming rage in his treatment of the body of Hektor. These last three books follow the same structural pattern in Achilles' rage that the first twenty books did. Achilles anger at Agamemnon is replaced with anger at Hektor. Likewise, just as Achilles reached a reconciliation with Agamemnon, so will he reconcile with Hektor's father, Priam.

Achilles had begun the desecration of Hektor's corpse at the end of Book XXII, and he continues it, both explicitly and implicitly, in Book XXIII. Achilles' rage cannot be abated, and the reader can no longer feel sympathy for the Achaian warrior. Homer created a largely sympathetic and understandable character in Hektor. Hektor may have gloried over the dead Patroklos, but he did not mutilate the body; so now, Achilles' actions go beyond the bounds of acceptability. Just as Achilles' anger toward Agamemnon turned into petulance, his anger at those who killed Patroklos turns into irrational fury.

Achilles anger is interrupted and tempered by two events in Book XXIII: the dream appearance of Patroklos and the funeral games. In both cases, the reader is allowed to see a more humane aspect of Achilles.

Literary Device

The ghost of Patroklos is one of only a few instances of supernatural occurrences in the *Iliad*, along with the constant references to the gods. Even in this instance, the ghost of Patroklos is more of a dream vision than a real visitation. As in so many other encounters in the *Iliad*, the ghost of Patroklos can also be interpreted as a psychological event—Achilles talking to himself. The ghost's request for burial follows the ancient Greek belief that the soul cannot rest without burial. The vision of the ghost also helps prepare the way for Achilles' reconciliation with Priam in the last book. Patroklos represents the more human and humane sides of Achilles' personality, and the appearance of the ghost has a decided softening effect on Achilles' wrath.

Similarly, the funeral ceremony and games show Achilles in a more favorable light. The funeral rites involve a procession of chariots, the cutting of hair as a sign of mourning, and various sacrifices, including both animals and humans (the Trojan captives).

The burial is followed by the games, thought to be patterned on real sporting events such as the Olympic contests, which were founded approximately at the time the *Iliad* was composed. The general consensus of critics and historians is that the first four contests made up a typical series of games—two-horse chariot race, boxing, wrestling, and the footrace. The other three games—the armored fight, discus throwing, and the archery—are thought to be later additions.

One interesting sidelight, proving that some things never change, is the boxer Epeus' comment. Before entering the match, he shouts, "I am the greatest!"

The games provide for a last review of the heroes of the Greek army. These characters, who have played the major roles throughout the poem, appear here for the final time. The games allow the reader to see them in a more civilized competition and provide a valedictory and farewell for the Greek warriors. Only Achilles appears in Book XXIV.

Glossary

cortege a ceremonial procession, such as at a funeral.

dirge a slow, sad song, poem, or musical composition expressing grief or mourning; lament.

funeral games athletic contests held as part of the ritual of an important warrior's funeral.

gold, two-handled urn a vase used to hold ashes and other remains of a dead warrior.

Olympiad the athletic contests held near Mount Olympos in honor of the gods. The funeral games of Patroklos seem to be based on the contests of the Olympiad.

Book XXIV

Summary

Nine days pass after the funeral, and on each of these days, Achilles ties the body of Hektor to his chariot and drags it around the barrow of Patroklos. The gods, however, continue to preserve the corpse so that it does not deteriorate or rot.

Zeus then holds a meeting of the gods where it is decided that Hektor's body will be redeemed and given a suitable burial. To make this possible, the gods order Thetis to explain to her son, Achilles, that it is the will of Zeus that he restore Hektor's body to Priam, Hektor's father.

Escorted by the god Hermes, Priam and an old servant enter the Achaian camp that night, unseen. Priam appeals to Achilles as a suppliant, reminding Achilles of the feelings that he has for his own dead father. Achilles is so moved by these reawakened memories of home and parents that he agrees to accept Priam's offer of ransom for Hektor's body. The two men, Achilles and Priam, each having his own sorrow, weep together. Then Achilles has dinner prepared and provides Priam with a bed for the night. He even oversees the preparations of Hektor's body and also grants the Trojans a 12-day truce so that they have sufficient time to conduct Hektor's funeral rites.

All the people of Troy come out to mourn Hektor's body. Andromache, Hekuba, and Helen, all of whom praise Hektor and describe their own reasons for regretting his death, lead the lamentations.

During the period of the truce, the Trojans gather wood in the mountains and burn Hektor's body on a large funeral pyre. His bones are then placed in a golden chest, which is buried in a shallow grave. Over this, a barrow is erected. Afterward, a great funeral banquet is served in Priam's palace.

Commentary

The wrath of Achilles is finally assuaged in Book XXIV. Many people have noted connections between the last Book and the first because both involve a father seeking the return of a child. Agamemnon's rejection of Chryses in Book I leads to all of the events of the *Iliad*. Achilles' kindness to Priam in Book XXIV ends the warrior's wrath and brings the work full circle—the war situation is not essentially different from the way it was at the start. With Hektor's burial accomplished and Achilles' death imminent, the great antagonists of the *Iliad* have been dealt with.

The events here are the final resolution of the dramatic story of the wrath, or the anger, of Achilles and its aftermath. Until now, Achilles has undergone no real change of heart and has learned no moral lesson from his experiences. His meeting with Hektor's father, Priam, however, is a crucial stage in his moral development. In their conversation, Achilles reveals the full depth of his affection for Patroklos and demonstrates his ability to understand another man's sorrow; the more humane and nobler side of his character begins to regain influence as he learns to accept reality and to have compassion for others. By finally relenting and restoring Hektor's body to Priam, Achilles obeys the will of the gods and experiences a partial moral rehabilitation. He is changed and chastened. But his brief flash of temper, when Priam exhibits a small degree of caution and suspicion, reveals that he still has many of his irrational traits.

The final scene of the *Iliad* is one of the most impressive contributions Homer made to the saga of Troy and Achilles. By concluding his poem with the rehabilitation of Achilles, rather than with the death of Achilles or the fall of Troy, he wrote the *Iliad* as a poetic composition with a high level of artistic balance and symbolic meaning. It begins with a wrong deed done by Agamemnon to a suppliant father (Chryses) and ends with a right deed done by Achilles, another victim of Agamemnon, to another suppliant father (Priam). The opening and closing episodes of the poem thus focus the reader's attention directly on its central theme—the personal development of Achilles.

Glossary

Hermes often called the Messenger God, he acted as the Guide, such as in Book XXIV, taking Priam to Achilles' tent.

Niobe Phrygian woman whose twelve children were killed by Apollo and Artemis. Niobe is usually associated with mourning and weeping.

omen a sign of impending doom. Natural events, such as the flight of an eagle, were often seen as omens.

ransom payment to make up for death or to secure the return of a dead body; sometimes referred to in the *Iliad* as "man money."

CHARACTER ANALYSES

Achilles

The greatest warrior in the Achaian army. The *Iliad* is about the Trojan War, but it is primarily about the war as it is affected by Achilles' wrath, or anger. Achilles is the main character, and his inaction, or withdrawal from the fighting, is crucial to the plot. He is a complex warrior who sometimes ignores the cultural norms of his society because he sees through some of its fallacies—in particular, he sees many of the faults in the often narrow and contradictory heroic code. Achilles is also the greatest warrior and fighter among the Achaians. He is invulnerable (except on the heel) because his mother dipped him in the River Styx as a baby. Furthermore, no warrior comes close to being his equal as a fighter.

Achilles has a strong sense of social order that in the beginning, manifests itself in his concern for the disorder in the Achaian camp; a deadly plague is destroying the soldiers, and Achilles wants to know the reason why. His king, Agamemnon, will not act, so Achilles decides to act: He calls for an assembly of the entire army. In doing this, Achilles upsets the order of protocol; only Agamemnon can decide to call an assembly, but Achilles does so to try to return order to the Achaian camp. He succeeds, partially. He finds out why the plague is killing hundreds of Achaian soldiers, but in the process, he creates disorder when it is revealed that Agamemnon is responsible for the deadly plague. Thus, Achilles' attempt to return order to the Achaian camp does little, ultimately, to establish order. Apollo lifts the plague, but after Achilles withdraws himself and his troops from the Achaian army, disorder still remains among the Achaians.

Agamemnon, of course, is as guilty of creating the ensuing disorder as Achilles is, but Achilles seems petulant and argumentative. He is undermining the little harmony that does exist. In his argument that Agamemnon receives all the best war prizes and does nothing to earn them, Achilles forgets the valuable prizes that he has received. His rage even causes him to almost attempt to kill Agamemnon, but the goddess Athena saves him from this deed.

It should be noted that Achilles does not leave the Achaian army without sufficient reason: Agamemnon demanded to have the maiden Briseis, Achilles' war prize, and Achilles saw this act as a parallel to Paris' kidnapping of Helen—he sees himself in the same position as Menelaos. Consequently, the quarrel between himself and Agamemnon is as righteous to him as is the war against the Trojans. But even after Agamemnon offers to return Briseis, along with numerous other gifts,

Achilles remains angry, indicating that one of Achilles' major character flaws is his excessive pride. The gifts that Agamemnon offers do not compensate for the public affront, the public insult Achilles believes he has suffered. A concern for gifts, the reader realizes, is far less important to Achilles than his concern for a proper, honored place in the world. After all, Agamemnon had previously given gifts and then taken them back. He could do so again, so the promise of more gifts is possibly an empty promise.

This idea of social status is in keeping with the heroic code by which Achilles has lived, but in his isolation, he comes to question the idea of fighting for glory alone because "A man dies still if he has done nothing." The idea developing in Achilles' mind is that the concept of home (or family) *and* the individual are both important to society and to a heroic warrior. (Hektor is the embodiment of this view.) Some critics see these ideas slowly developing through Achilles' ability to relate to others on a personal basis, as he does with Patroklos, and as he does in his guest-host relationship with the ambassadors from Agamemnon.

However, it is only after Patroklos' death that these relationships and broader concepts of love begin to become significant for Achilles. Ironically, with the death of Patroklos, Achilles begins to see life and relationships with other people from a *mortal* point of view, and at the same time, he is drawing ever closer to the *divine* aspects of love. He has an obligation to avenge Patroklos' death, and he realizes his own shortcomings as Patroklos' protector. He also sees that his sitting by his ships is "a useless weight on the good land," something that is causing the deaths of many Achaian warriors. Unfortunately, however, Achilles is unable to see that the Achaians feel his withdrawal as keenly as he now feels the loss of Patroklos.

It is Achilles' anger, whether he is sulking or whether he is violent, that is paramount throughout most of the epic. In fact, his battle with the river is probably one of the most savage scenes in the *Iliad*. It shows us Achilles' insane wrath at its height. On first reading, the scene may seem confusing, but it is important to the reader's view of Achilles and to the mutilation theme. Mutilation of bodies and Achilles' excesses prompt the river god to charge him with excessive evil. He charges Achilles with not merely killing, but "outraging the corpse."

Homer so vividly personifies the river god that he describes the battle between them as being a battle between two beings, even though, at the same time, it is a vivid description of a man caught in a flood, literally fighting for his life. If the reader can visualize this scene, seeing a thick debris of trees, powerful rocks, and strong waves lashing against Achilles, the scene becomes more powerful and meaningful.

Achilles has over-reached himself, and as he attempts to punish all the Trojans for Patroklos' death and to deny them burial rites for Hektor, so the river god now attempts to drown Achilles, bury him in the mud, and deny *him* glory and proper burial rites. It is also significant that the river god is the only god to confront Achilles with excessive cruelty and lack of pity. Later, however, the other gods come to view Achilles as the river god does.

Achilles' violence closes with the death of Hektor and with Achilles' mutilation of Hektor's corpse. By now, under Zeus' firm hand, the gods have moved from their own state of disorder to order. When the gods see Achilles act without any sense of pity for Hektor or his family, they come back into Zeus' all-wise fold of authority. And eventually, through his mother, Thetis, even Achilles is finally persuaded to accede to Zeus' will. In the end, Achilles is exhausted. His passions are spent, and he consents to give up Hektor's corpse.

Patroklos

Even though Patroklos is an important character in the *Iliad*, Homer gives little attention to him until the ninth book, and even then, the focus is not on Patroklos himself, but on his relationship to Achilles. In fact, one rarely sees Patroklos as an individual. There is no dramatic character development, but one does see Patroklos as a character perpetrates dramatic events and provides a clearer understanding of Achilles. Patroklos' main purpose in the *Iliad* is to bring Achilles back into the war. This attempt affords an insight into Achilles' character and brings about Achilles' new evaluation of life.

Although one sees Patroklos' strengths and weaknesses (his "aristeia") during his battle scenes, Homer uses him primarily to move the plot along and to highlight the actions and thoughts of other characters.

Achilles and Patroklos have a particularly close relationship, based partly upon the heroic code of warrior-companion and partly upon Patroklos' role as an advisor to Achilles. While certain customs must be followed in such relationships, the spirit of the code is of greater importance to these two warriors. Homer demonstrates the heroic and familiar love between the two men and the obvious bond of mutual respect extending beyond the warrior-companion relationship.

Patroklos makes no speeches in the *Iliad*. When he and Achilles are together, before Agamemnon's ambassadors arrive, Patroklos waits for Achilles to finish singing before he begins speaking. When Agamemnon's agents arrive, Patroklos silently mixes drinks, and then both he and Achilles work together as equals to prepare a meal for the guests. Each one seems to understand the thoughts and desires of the other. It is as though Patroklos is Achilles' alter ego, or "second self," an idea that carries over into Patroklos' aristeia.

Later, after Patroklos has returned from Nestor's camp, his deep sensitivity to the Achaian losses and the death of his friends is apparent. When he asks Achilles' permission to enter the war, Achilles compares him to a "silly little girl," and while Achilles' comment underscores Patroklos' obedient sensitivity, it also indicates Patroklos' dependence upon Achilles and shows a strong emotional bond that activates Achilles' wrath after Patroklos' death. But the emotional interdependence between the two men does *not* prevent Patroklos from criticizing Achilles' anger, and at one point, asking *who* can cure Achilles' consuming wrath. Patroklos even tells Achilles that he hopes that he himself is never cursed with such anger.

Patroklos may be, in a sense, Achilles' alter ego, or "second self," but his error is in believing that he can perform as brilliantly as Achilles on the battlefield. When he puts on Achilles' armor, he tries to assume Achilles' identity, and as a result, he tries a feat that is beyond his own strength. That is, Patroklos tries to lead the Achaian attack on the city of Troy, despite the fact that Achilles has warned him not to attempt to do anything except protect the Achaian fleet of ships.

In three drives into the Trojan front, Patroklos kills nine men in each drive, but on the fourth drive, Apollo strikes him across the back, sending him into a daze and making him vulnerable to Hektor's attack. As Patroklos is dying, he is aware that he is a scapegoat and that it was not Hektor, but Apollo who was his "deadly destiny," because Apollo inspired him to attack the wall even though Achilles had instructed him specifically not to do so. Patroklos thus realizes that by taking Achilles' place in battle, he has become the means by which Achilles' return to the war is assured. He reminds Hektor that "death and powerful destiny are standing beside" him. Destiny, then, guides Patroklos from the moment he enters the war.

After killing Patroklos, Hektor deviates from the code of honor by threatening to give Patroklos' body to the dogs. Patroklos' death thereby leads to the deaths of both Hektor and Achilles in the sense that both dishonor Greek ideals by threats and acts of desecration.

Agamemnon

Agamemnon inherited the role of king from his father, and his community expects him, as king, to stabilize society, arbitrate disputes, and call council meetings and assemblies. He is also commander-in-chief of the armies. Both Odysseus and old Nestor (two of his commanders) attempt to maintain Agamemnon's authority because they recognize that supporting Agamemnon is the only way to ensure an effective and meaningful policy of order. Agamemnon is, after all, the king and their leader.

Yet despite that Agamemnon is king and has enormous power and social position, he is not necessarily the best qualified for the role. Old Nestor frequently advises Agamemnon because Agamemnon needs counsel. Almost immediately, the reader sees that Agamemnon often allows his over-wrought emotions to govern major, critical decisions. Nestor advises Agamemnon against taking Briseis from Achilles, but Agamemnon doesn't listen, thereby setting up a chain of events that results in the deaths of hundreds of Achaian soldiers.

Unfortunately, Agamemnon was born to a role greater than his ability, and Achilles, another hot-tempered Greek, was born to a role less than his ability. Both men are great men, but both are quick to anger, and both are conscious of the roles that they must play within the heroic code. Neither man is willing to compromise or to accept a seemingly lower status within the heroic code, and so their quarrel over Briseis results in a tragic breach between the two—one that creates a central conflict in the *Iliad*.

Note, however, that Agamemnon shows devotion to and concern for his brother, Menelaos. Agamemnon realizes that order in the Achaian society depends upon Helen's return to Menelaos. He is aware of the importance of *family order* if all of society is to remain cohesive. Yet with all these good traits, Agamemnon is plagued with other traits that undermine his good qualities and contribute to self-created problems.

Agamemnon is weak; he vacillates. During periods of depression and discouragement, he makes wrong decisions, and he is sometimes unfair. He fails to realize that a king must *not* succumb to his own desires and emotions. He does not realize that authority demands responsibility and that his personal wishes must be *secondary* to the needs of the community. His failure to understand the limitations of power causes him to make his first error: He *insists* on keeping his Trojan war prize, Chryseis, despite her father's pleas. He likes her, and he believes that he will lose face if he returns her.

Eventually, Agamemnon learns to listen to the counsel of old Nestor, Odysseus, and Diomedes, but it seems clear that his emotional makeup and inability to judge do not fully qualify him for kingship. Even after he finally admits to his madness in dealing with Achilles and attempts to reverse the error with gifts and the return of Briseis, he only insults Achilles. When his courage flags and he becomes depressed, he wants to abandon the Trojan War altogether.

Despite Agamemnon's prowess as a warrior, as a king he too often exhibits the characteristics of stubbornness, cowardice, and immaturity. As the reader carefully studies Agamemnon's character, some growth in understanding can be seen in him particularly in Book IX when he sends the embassy to Achilles. At the end of the epic, Agamemnon is a much greater leader than in the early books, even though he never reaches the same stature as several of the other warriors.

Odysseus

Homer uses Odysseus' stability and maturity as a foil to both Achilles and Agamemnon. There is no character development in Odysseus, but his purpose in the *Iliad* does not call for dramatic character development. His purpose is to show us strong demonstrations of tact, strategic ability, and heroic capability, all of which are qualities that a king should have. Additionally, Homer also shows Odysseus' ability to advise. Above all, Odysseus exhibits self-control, and a *lack* of self-control is alarmingly apparent in both Achilles and Agamemnon. It is also obvious that Odysseus has greater kingly qualifications than Agamemnon because his decisions are almost always sound and successful when followed. He is always rational and diplomatic.

For example, as one of Agamemnon's ambassadors to Achilles, Odysseus presents Agamemnon's offers. But when Achilles refuses to accept the offers, Odysseus does not argue with Achilles. He knows that arguing with Achilles is useless, and by arguing, he may defeat the purpose of the mission and force Achilles into an even stronger position of alienation from the Achaian forces. Further, when confronted with Achilles' angry desire to rush into battle after the death of Patroklos, Odysseus calmly argues that the army must eat first. Homer almost always refers to Odysseus as the "great tactician" and it is Odysseus who eventually comes up with the stratagem of the Trojan Horse that wins the war.

As a foil to both Achilles and Agamemnon, Odysseus' ability to remain calm and analyze a problem stands out boldly against both men's quickness to anger and their inability to resolve their differences tactfully.

By continually supporting order over disorder, Odysseus acts as a stabilizing factor in the *Iliad,* and even Homer's comments about Odysseus' cunning do not detract from his heroic stature.

Nestor

Nestor's place in the *Iliad* is important because he is a wise counselor and because he motivates the plot. Some critics see him as a ridiculous figure, and it cannot be denied that he is at times a comic figure; but Nestor's digressive tales frequently motivate a character to perform some necessary action or reveal relevant cultural ideas. His tales are usually paradigmatic (showing parallels by examples) and serve as examples for present situations.

The modern reader may see Nestor as garrulous and unnecessary, or as a useless adjunct to the Achaian army; but the Greeks did not view him as such. He is the oldest man among the Achaians, and the Greeks saw advantages in old age. They believed that an elder man knew more, and here, the Achaians listen to the wisdom that old Nestor has gained through age. Consequently, Nestor's tales and advice serve to challenge younger men to live up to heroic ideals that he himself upheld in the past.

Nestor challenges the Achaians to fight Hektor by saying to them that if he were younger, he would fight Hektor. To prove his former prowess, he tells the story of his fight with Ereuthalion in the Pylian war, a circumstance similar to the present war. The tale prompts nine warriors to "stand forth" to fight Hektor. Here, again, the wisdom of Nestor is useful in that he has the men draw lots. The disorder caused by Hektor's challenge has become ordered through Nestor's example.

Nestor's stories always have a purpose, and the story he tells Patroklos is intended to bring Achilles back into the war. It is a story of disorder brought about by Herakles and restored by Nestor's efforts. The tale points out that the Achaians need a leader and that Achilles should return to battle to save the Achaians. While Nestor is unsuccessful in bringing Achilles back into the war, he convinces Patroklos that Achilles' Myrmidon troops are necessary for the Achaians' success.

However, Homer uses Nestor as more than a counselor, and he uses Nestor's tales as more than a means to encourage the warriors to action. Nestor's tales enrich the epic with stories of the past that connect the past to the present and reveal a continuity of Greek life and hence Greek literature. There are links to the *Odyssey* and the *Iliad*. Nestor becomes the transmitter of memory, which is critical for the immortality of their heroes.

In all of Nestor's speeches, his purpose is to motivate an individual or a group to action. He first attempts to settle the quarrel between Achilles and Agamemnon. Second, he advises the Achaians to build a wall, and afterward, to bury their dead. Third, he suggests the spy mission. Fourth, he advises Agamemnon to send goodwill ambassadors to Achilles with gifts. And fifth, he inspires Patroklos to persuade Achilles to return to battle. He proves to be a wise counselor, and most of those whom he counsels recognize his wisdom.

During the funeral games, Achilles presents a gift to Nestor in respect for his old age. In turn, Nestor prays that Achilles enjoys a similar happiness. One critic suggests that through his respect for Nestor, Achilles is later able to recognize the value of Priam, Hektor's father. Likewise, the early prowess of Nestor seems to parallel Achilles' prowess.

Nestor's ability to soothe hard feelings, to use praise as a means for motivation, and to make tactful suggestions to a king are all acquired through experience. Only Odysseus equals Nestor in his ability to bring order out of disorder.

Hektor

Hektor is the undisputed commander of the Trojan army. No other Trojan warrior approaches Hektor's courage and valor. He is also viewed as the future king of Troy, and as such, he already shows his responsibility to the community. His concern for the Trojan women and for the Trojan community in general define him as a "norm" for Homeric society.

Unwittingly, however, Hektor (the Trojans' best warrior) acts as an agent to bring back Achilles (the Achaians' best warrior) into battle, because after Hektor kills Patroklos, Achilles believes that he has no choice except to revenge Patroklos by killing Hektor. As a result, Hektor will shortly become the victim of Achilles. But it should be stressed that Hektor is *trapped* by the illusion of a Trojan victory, a victory that was seemingly guaranteed by Zeus himself. That is, Hektor continues a fight that everyone, including himself, knows is doomed by fate because he grasps at the illusion of Trojan victory.

Throughout the epic, Hektor functions largely as a comparison and contrast (or a foil) to Achilles. As a mature man with a family and with strong feelings about his responsibilities, Hektor is a contrast to Achilles' frustrations and passionate outbursts of emotion. Hektor has dedicated his life to the service of others; he is an example of a "model" Homeric man. In contrast, Achilles seems superhuman because of his extremes and excesses. However, both are great warriors and the leading soldiers on their respective sides.

In addition to Hektor's social responsibilities and his heroic qualities, he is also a thoughtful commander. He focuses his energy; and although he fears Telamonian Aias (Ajax), he bravely battles with him until nightfall. Virtuous and faithful to the gods in all respects, he refuses the wine that his mother, Hekuba, offers him because he is tired and unclean and he fears that wine may cause him to forget his duty to his troops.

An example of Hektor's concern for virtue is evident when he rebukes Paris for kidnapping Helen, the act that perpetrated the war. He refers to Paris' act as shameful. Paris' behavior places Hektor in a dilemma: It is socially necessary to protect Paris, but it is also morally and socially correct to rebuke him. Thus, the heroic code binds Hektor into an uncomfortable, untenable position.

Helen also places Hektor in an untenable position, and her being a woman complicates the problem. Helen is a guest at the Trojan court, and she is also the wife of Paris. Paris also pirated some of Menelaos' material treasures, but the fact remains that Helen is still a wife without a dowry, a matter that runs counter to Troy's social codes. Hektor does not blame Helen; but being improperly married, she is a symbol of disorder and a threat to the social systems of both the Trojans and the Achaians.

Unlike Helen, Hektor's wife Andromache is associated with social order and the continuation of the family. Hektor's obvious love for Andromache symbolizes his belief in proper domesticity, and his image of her being taken captive and working the loom for another man represents his deep fear of disorder. Hektor also expresses concern that

Andromache might be taken captive by the Greeks, suggesting that he sees, through Helen, the wrong that Paris committed.

Hektor's relationship and attitude toward women and children is deeply embedded in Homeric culture. In the code of that era, the son fights like his father, but the son is also raised by his mother, and she teaches him that he must be a hero, fighting for her and for other women who will also raise heroes. In this culture, there was a great concern for women, because they were dependent and, like young children, they were vulnerable to enslavement. As a hero, then, Hektor is not only an extension of his father, he is also an extension of his mother, and when she begs him to come into the city of Troy, she assumes the position of a suppliant, appealing for mercy on the battlefield. Hektor's choice to remain on the battlefield and fight Achilles in a duel ignores her plea; therefore, in accordance with the idea that the hero is an extension of the mother, Hektor will be guilty of her death if anything happens to her. Priam's plea to his son is similar to Hekuba's, but his plea is for family continuity and for Troy.

An important idea in the *Iliad* is how "the plan, or will of Zeus" affects Hektor. The god's promise to Thetis (to give victory to the Trojans) traps Hektor into a key role. Zeus has promised him divine help with victory that will last until the Trojans have reached the beaches and the Achaian ships. Hektor assumes that final victory is his. Of course, though, it isn't. Therefore, Hektor can be seen as an instrument of Zeus. But although he is an instrument of Zeus, he is not a victim of Zeus. Hektor has sufficient flaws and errors to cause him to deserve his death. With this in mind, one must ask, "What is Hektor's error?"

An "error" is a misdeed *consciously* committed, and as such, a character must live with the shame of having committed the deed. Error sometimes occurs when the hero seeks only honor. If a warrior is reliable, he is admired, and if others admire the warrior, then he admires himself. According to the heroic code, the warrior should gain his honor by combat; consequently, he often over-reaches himself in his attempt to win honor. In the case of Hektor, it is sometimes difficult to determine what Hektor does in full knowledge, which constitutes an error, and what he does when he is acting as an instrument of the gods.

Hektor's first error is his *promise* to his fellow Trojans of a Trojan victory after the Achaians have been driven back to their ships. In his speech, he announces his plan for the Trojan troops to remain on the plain, ready for an early attack. The Trojan victory, however, is a result of his misunderstanding Zeus' plan which is simply to give the Trojans success until they reach the Greek ships so that the Achaians, specifically Agamemnon, will be punished for the mistreatment of Achilles. Hektor's success in battle, then, leads to a presumptuous *wish for immortality* and, consequently, to the beginning of Hektor's deterioration.

Hektor's second error is his *refusal* to withdraw his troops back to the city, as Poulydamas advises. Hektor is fired with victory and with Zeus' promise of aid. As soon as his troops reach the ships, Hektor's re-enforcement from Zeus is at an end. Hektor's gravest error, of course, occurs when he *refuses* to take refuge within the Trojan walls.

Homer shows us a portrait of Hektor as a leader concerned for Troy and its people and as a man who believes strongly in the cultural code of his community. Within Troy itself, Hektor reacts to social conditions in accordance with a heroic sense of order. Leaving the city, he becomes blinded by his military successes, by his own strength, and by the delusion that Zeus totally supports the Trojan cause. On the battlefield, Hektor is less responsive to individuals than he was within the walls of Troy; he does not seem to be the same Hektor portrayed earlier in the epic. The process of isolation has begun, and it ends with Hektor's complete isolation, outside of the walls of Troy, battling with Achilles until one of them is dead.

When Hektor kills Patroklos, his self-delusion is in full stride. Unknown to Hektor, Apollo, as Asios, goads Hektor into fighting Patroklos, saying, "You might be able to kill him. Apollo might give you such glory." Thus, Hektor becomes the instrument of *both* Zeus and Apollo, for as Patroklos tells Hektor, Zeus and Apollo conquered him, not Hektor. Hektor is only Patroklos' *third* slayer.

Hektor's deterioration becomes even more evident when he violates the heroic code of honor. He threatens to drag Patroklos' body back to Troy and throw it to the "dogs of the city" instead of allowing the Achaians to give it an honorable burial. Hektor's treatment of Patroklos' body, in turn, prompts Achilles to mutilate Hektor's body.

When Hektor puts on Achilles' armor, he becomes as erratic as Achilles in his quarrel with Agamemnon. Achilles' armor covers Hektor's true identity to a degree that it brings about Hektor's death.

The reader pities Hektor as he meets Achilles in the final duel, yet his deterioration, his lack of self-knowledge, and his self-delusion have brought him to this final reckoning with Achilles. Hektor fails to maintain a heroic balance when he overestimates his powers and refuses to retreat when necessary. As he meets Achilles, he stands deluded by a dream of invisibility. Physically and symbolically isolated outside his community, he is cut down by Achilles.

Hektor is a more complicated figure than most of the other characters in the *Iliad*. His responsibility to Troy, to his troops, to his family, and to the moral and heroic code, and his role as the instrument of Zeus set up tensions that no other character seems to experience. Hektor may appear to be a warrior with greater military prowess than most warriors, but he also seems to be an uncomplicated Homeric man. It is, therefore, Hektor's various interrelationships and his multiple responsibilities that bring out the various and often contradictory facets of his character.

Priam

When King Priam and Helen are on the Trojan ramparts, and Helen is describing the leaders of the Achaian forces to him, Priam is able to distinguish the kingly aspects of Agamemnon. He envies Agamemnon for his position as a "warrior-king," calling him a "blessed child of fortune and favor." As king of the Trojans, Priam is bothered by his not having a duality of roles. Agamemnon, it seems, has the best of both worlds; he is both a warrior and a king. Priam is only a king. He is no longer a warrior, and he must depend upon his son Hektor for prowess, as well as for continuing the kingship of Troy. In Priam's speech from the wall, before Hektor's duel with Achilles, the reader has a glimpse of Priam's torn feelings for Hektor, as well as his vision of Troy's destruction. Priam knows that Hektor is the only force that can save Troy, and if Achilles kills Hektor, then Priam cannot preserve his family or his city. As a king, he *must* use Hektor's "force," his warrior prowess to save Troy; as a father, though, Priam realizes that if his "force" is destroyed, he will lose a son.

As one critic points out, Hektor symbolizes Troy's security, and he *must* fight to remain the "symbol of Trojan stability." Priam knows this. He must act as king to save his city, but in doing so, he *must* sacrifice a son. Priam knows that Troy's destruction is imminent, and as a father, he does not want to sacrifice his son for a lost cause.

Watching Achilles abuse Hektor's body, Priam bemoans the loss of so many sons whom Achilles has cut down, but of all the sons whom he has lost, he mourns most for Hektor. Wishing that Hektor might have died in his arms is a wish for a stable society, one in which the family functions as a microcosm of society. At the same time, Priam realizes that by overprotecting his son Paris, he undermined the social fabric of Troy. His error led to Hektor's death, his only son with a sense of social order.

Hekuba, Priam's wife, fears for her husband's safety when he tells her that he is going to Achilles' camp; she does not believe that the gods will protect Priam, but he is adamant about going. He has seen the goddess Iris, and he trusts her message. He warns Hekuba not to be a "bird of bad omen in my palace." Furthermore, if it is to be his *destiny* to die beside the Achaian ships, then so be it. Before leaving, and at Hekuba's suggestion, Priam purifies himself; he asks for a sign, and Zeus sends a black eagle to give Priam assurance that his mission has divine approval.

Priam's journey to Achilles' camp takes on a surreal, dream-like quality as Priam and his herald leave. Darkness descends while they water the horses at a river, and the scene seems to suggest a journey to the underworld; in fact, Zeus sends Hermes to conduct Priam to Achilles' camp. The appearance of Hermes gives the impression that Priam is symbolically "crossing over" (symbolically, entering Hades) as he goes to meet Achilles, who also symbolically "crosses over" to meet Priam. As a result, both men discover new spiritual values by exploring the spiritual world. Priam specifically learns a kind of humility in going alone to plead for the body of his son. He also seems able to face the certainty of future ruin because he has succeeded on a personal level with Achilles.

Until Priam comes to him, Achilles has felt sympathy for *no one,* except Patroklos. Priam's visit gives both men an understanding of the common bonds of humanity.

Priam follows Iris' instructions of going to Achilles as a suppliant, where he plays the role of a father and not that of king of Troy. Were Priam to go to Achilles as king of Troy, the meeting would be purely for negotiating, and neither Achilles nor Priam would gain spiritually from the encounter. However, going as a suppliant, Priam falls into the category of a guest-friend, and as such, Achilles receives him as the father of Hektor. Kissing Achilles' hands, Priam lays aside his kingly role and pleads with Achilles to remember his own father, who is also old. Priam says that his sons are dead and the only son who could help him (that is, Hektor) now lies dead in Achilles' camp. Priam adds that he has kissed the hands of the man who killed his children. By kissing Achilles' hands instead of *avenging* Hektor's death, Priam breaks a taboo, and by this act, Priam humbles himself before Achilles.

Priam's act causes Achilles to see Priam as he sees his own father, and the awakening of sympathy within Achilles begins. While Priam mourns for Hektor, Achilles mourns for what his father will endure when he, Achilles, is dead. By their mourning together, Achilles' wrath becomes anguish, and Priam's anguish becomes forgiveness. Together, the two men form a special kinship through suffering.

Through their mutual suffering, Priam and Achilles leave the social sphere of the Homeric world behind and enter the divine sphere of human understanding. With new insight, Achilles begins his purification; he begins anew to understand his world and his relationship to the world and its social mores. As Priam's character is reviewed, one sees a figure for whom she can feel much sympathy. There is often the feeling that he does not deserve all that happens to him. Priam is apparently a good man who follows social norms and who worships the gods as he should. However, his son Paris presents a problem when he asks his father to condone the violation of a social norm by kidnapping a married Greek woman and thus violating the concept of "hospitality is obligatory." By forcing Priam to accept Helen into his own house, Paris causes Priam to accept the wrong Paris committed. Paris' action tests the social norm of the Trojans and ultimately brings total destruction to Priam's family, to the whole social structure of Troy, and to Troy itself. What Paris did was wrong. But no one can say that Priam himself is evil; it can be said, simply, that he was unwise to violate a social norm so fraught with contradictions that *no answer* other than total destruction was possible.

CRITICAL ESSAYS

The Hero and Homeric Culture

The notion of personal honor is prevalent throughout the *Iliad*. The honor of every person in Homeric culture was important, but to the hero, his honor was paramount. He could not endure insults, and he felt that he had to protect his reputation—even unto death. The hero's duty was to fight, and the only way he had of gaining glory and immortality was through heroic action on the battlefield; thus, he continually prepared his life for the life-and-death risks of battle. The Homeric hero believed that men had to stand together in battle; men had to respect each other; and they had to refrain from excessive cruelty. This last condition was critically important for the Homeric hero. He loathed deliberate acts of cruelty and injustice. If he were ready to kill a victim, he believed that he should do it quickly; he was not to mutilate him, as Achilles does with Hektor's body. By following this code, a hero gained a sense of dignity and a reputation for honor that would ensure his place in the social memory of his community.

TheHomeric hero lived by strict social and cultural norms that would guide his life at home and on the battlefield. His position as a hero depended upon understanding his place in society and performing in accordance with society's expectations. He accepted the pattern of a hero, which included a hero's suffering and a hero's death. When the hero expressed himself in words, he believed that his thoughts were derived from either society or a god. Nothing came from within. (In his soliloquies, the hero speaks to "his own great-hearted spirit" as though it were another person helping him make the right decisions.)

Communal honor was vital to the Homeric hero's status; his whole world revolved around his relationship with his family and city. If he lost the personal honor or glory that was accorded him by his community, he felt that life had lost its meaning. Achilles, for example, feels that he has lost his honor when Agamemnon takes Briseis from him. He feels a sense of rejection, and even Agamemnon's later offer of gifts in order to bring Achilles back to the fighting is futile because Achilles realizes that he will lose even more honor if he accepts Agamemnon's gifts.

The hero's social responsibility was essential to maintain his status, but the only way to establish his status was through his performance as a hero in combat on the battlefield. Furthermore, he had to show respect for and respond to social situations and mores; he had to respect his superiors and show loyalty to his friends, and he could in no way disgrace himself, his family, or his community. However, it was no disgrace to withdraw from an impossible situation because it was all a warrior could do at times. Patroklos, however, forgets this principle, as well as Achilles' warning not to drive the Trojans back to their city. Patroklos fails because he becomes irrational and allows pride to overcome his reason.

The Homeric community depended upon their heroes to defend its social and religious rites and all other facets of community life. Being a hero was a social responsibility that entitled a man to social status, and a warrior defined and justified his social status only on the battlefield.

The hero in Homeric culture recognized the rightness of his community's anger. For example, when Agamemnon strips Achilles of his war prize, Agamemnon places the responsibility for his actions on Zeus and Destiny. He says, "It is the god who accomplishes all things" and he claims that "Delusion" entangled him. Similarly, when Achilles ponders whether or not to draw his sword against Agamemnon, Athena grabs him by the hair and warns him against fighting with Agamemnon. Clearly, Achilles does not assume responsibility either for his anger or for his not killing Agamemnon. In fact, neither Achilles nor Agamemnon recognizes a personal responsibility for their emotional and physical responses, even though both men are on the edge of violence. To the Homeric hero, an outside force initiates action and thought—hence, personal responsibility is not an issue for a hero's decision to follow the dictates of an outside force.

A hero always had two choices: He could follow an external force, or he could make his own personal decisions. This idea derives from the concept that a man became a hero because he possessed certain qualities. Among those qualities is heroic balance, which requires a hero to insist upon his greatness and maintain a proper modesty before the gods. He had to know himself and be able to evaluate and act upon a situation. He also had to recognize the time when the gods withdrew their help, and at that time the hero had to withdraw from battle. If he failed to recognize how much his action was ruled by the gods, he lost his heroic balance and made a tragic error. If he failed to follow the gods and made his own decisions, he had to live with the shame of his mistake, and when he erred, he lost approval and honor.

The hero's fear of disgrace (*aidos*) governed his response to all social situations and to the judgements of others. If he acted incorrectly, society would scorn him. Yet despite the threat of others' judgements note the actions of both Agamemnon and Achilles during the quarrel in Book I. Both men are at fault. Agamemnon breaks the bond of hero and community by insulting Achilles and claiming Briseis in lieu of

Chryseis. Likewise, Achilles' threat to kill Agamemnon is a social act which, if carried out, would not only show disrespect for his superiors, but would force his Achaian community of soldiers to leave Troy. The disorder that is created by this crisis demands a restoration of order.

Heroes were constantly in fear of disgrace; they feared the judgement of their community. The hero did not distinguish between personal morals and conformity to the morals of the greater society; he concerned himself wholly with acceptance by the people, for if he failed to conform in any way, he risked the anger of his community and, consequently, shame.

Theme I: Anger, Strife, Alienation, and Reconciliation

The main theme of the *Iliad* is stated in the first line, as Homer asks the Muse to sing of the "wrath of Achilles." This wrath, all its permutations, transformations, influences, and consequences, makes up the themes of the *Iliad.* In essence, the wrath of Achilles allows Homer to present and develop, within the cultural framework of heroic honor (see Critical Essay 1), the ideas of strife, alienation, and reconciliation.

The wrath of Achilles is provoked by Achilles' sense of honor as a result of *eris* or discord, which leads to the warrior's alienation from the Greeks and eventually from human society. Second, the wrath of Achilles sets him up in clear contrast to his great Trojan counterpart in the story—Hektor. Finally, the assuaging of Achilles' wrath leads to the reconciliation and reintegration of the warrior, first into his own community and second into the larger community of all humanity. When considering these three basic ideas that result from the wrath of Achilles, readers can see a grand design in the work that centers not so much on war as on the growth and development of an individual character.

Achilles wrath is initiated by his sense of honor. Honor for the Greeks, and specifically heroes, as readers have seen, existed on different levels. First, arete: the pursuit of excellence. Second, nobility: on the personal level, men had to treat each other properly; personal regard and honor from one's peers was essential to the proper functioning of society. Third, valor: obtained by a warrior for his accomplishments in battle. Fourth, and finally, the Greeks could obtain everlasting fame and glory for their accomplishments in life. The wrath of Achilles is based on each of these concepts.

Underlying the idea of honor is another Greek concept—strife, personified by the goddess Eris. For the Greeks, life was based on the idea of strife and turmoil. To try to avoid strife was to avoid life. A good life could be achieved by reconciling the factors that produced strife. However, war, nature, personality—everything—contained elements of strife that may not be completely reconcilable. This more elemental strife could lead to evil. Both types of strife are involved in Achilles' anger.

In a most significant way, Achilles' life begins with an attempt to avoid strife. His parents, the goddess Thetis and the mortal Peleus, invite all the gods to their wedding except Eris (strife). Eris, however, like the evil witch in fairy tales, attends anyway and tosses out the golden apple marked, "For the Fairest." Thus, strife enters at the wedding of Achilles' parents and sets in motion the events that will ultimately lead to the Trojan War.

On a more personal level, Achilles himself is an embodiment of stressful opposites. One parent is mortal; one a goddess. Consequently, he knows both mortality and immortality. He knows he must die, but he also has a sense of the eternal. He knows that if he avoids the war he can live a long life, but that if he fights, he will die young. He knows that glory and eternal fame can be his only through early death in war while long life can be secured only by giving up the ultimate glory a Greek seeks. At first, Achilles attempts to avoid the Trojan War by pretending to be a woman; but, as in a number of instances, his attempts to avoid an action lead directly to that action.

In the *Iliad*, Achilles' initial anger is a direct result of an act that Achilles perceives to be an attack on his personal honor. Agamemnon takes Briseis from Achilles. In response, Achilles withdraws from the war, producing greater strife, both personally and within the larger context of the war. Achilles cannot reconcile his desire to fight honorably with his companions with his justifiable, but increasingly petulant, anger at Agamemnon. Moreover, Achilles' withdrawal produces the real strife of war, as the Trojans, emboldened by the absence of Achilles, attack the Greeks and their ships with increasing ferocity and success.

As a result of his inner conflict, his alienation from his society, and his inability to resolve this conflict, Achilles sends his companion Patroklos into battle as an alter ego. Patroklos even wears the armor of Achilles so that the Trojans will believe that Achilles has returned to battle. Patroklos is killed, and the turmoil within Achilles is magnified. Achilles sent Patroklos into battle instead of going himself; now he bears responsibility for the death of his friend. Also, now the Trojans are so empowered that they appear poised to win the conflict with the Greeks.

At this point, Achilles resolves the strife that led to his initial wrath but also begins the even greater wrath that results in the death of Hektor and almost takes Achilles beyond the bounds of humanity. Achilles is torn by his own responsibilities in the death of Patroklos and his hatred of the Trojans, specifically Hektor, who actually killed Patroklos. In the last five books of the *Iliad*, this conflict is transformed into the superhuman rage that Achilles displays as a warrior. After killing Hektor, Achilles allows his rage to move beyond death to desecration as he mutilates, time and again, the corpse of Hektor. At this point, Achilles is on the threshold of complete alienation from human feelings. Only through the recognition of his own kinship with both the living and the dead is he able to finally resolve the conflict and strife that has motivated his rage.

Reconciliation ends the wrath of Achilles and makes him more than a warrior hero. Achilles' anger occurs in two great waves. The first wave, his withdrawal from battle because of conflict with Agamemnon, ends when Achilles accepts Agamemnon's offer and reaches agreement concerning Briseis. Achilles' second wave of anger is over the death of Patroklos and ends when Achilles returns Hektor's body to Priam.

In both these instances, Achilles' wrath has alienated him from those around him. In the first case, he becomes alienated from the other Achaians, his companions in battle; in the second, from humanity in general. In each case, Achilles achieves a reconciliation that allows him to be reintegrated into both his the heroic community and the larger community of humanity. Even so, Achilles remains a hero who is not easily understood. He becomes accepted, and even admired, but never quite comprehendible in the way Hektor is. Through the process of reconciliation, Achilles becomes a memorable literary hero like Oedipus or Beowulf or Hamlet: heroic and noble, but still somehow apart from others, somehow different.

Through reconciliation, Achilles achieves a tragic dimension. If Achilles does not return to the battle, his anger would be nothing more than petulant selfishness. His return, and knowing that he will die in the war, makes him not only a hero but also a hero touched with tragedy. If Achilles does not return Hektor's body to the distraught Priam, then his wrath concerning Patroklos and toward Hektor's corpse would be nothing more than the rage of mindless vengeance. His kindness toward Priam, recognizing his own kinship with the dead and defeated, makes him not only a tragic hero but also an existential one.

The fact that Achilles does recognize his kinship with those he has killed is what raises the *Iliad* to the level of existential tragedy. This recognition of kinship by Achilles begins in Book XXII. Before he kills Lykaon, Achilles says, "Come friend, you too must die." Most commentators have seen this scene as a sublime moment in the poem in which Achilles asserts the inevitability of death and suggests a kinship between Lykaon, Patroklos, himself, and all the other warriors who have died or will die in battle. This recognition of death is similar to the recognition by Meursault, in *The Stranger*, that his execution, his death, is the bond that connects him to all humanity. Like Meursault, Achilles is an estranged person, and his acceptance of the inevitability of death is his ultimate assertion of a common bond with all humanity.

This notion of accepting death reaches its zenith when Achilles returns the body of Hektor to Priam. During the last few books of the *Iliad*, Achilles becomes more and more aware of his own impending death. Even as he rages against Hektor's corpse, he sees his own demise foreshadowed. At the funeral games he rejoins his fellow Achaians. And with Priam, he rejoins the circle of humanity.

That words such as *alienation*, *existential*, and *tragedy* can be used to describe the *Iliad* demonstrates the greatness of Homer's achievement. The ideas that underlie the *Iliad* are the ideas that underlie all great literature. Interestingly, the first great hero of Western Literature is also the first modern hero of Western Literature.

Theme II: The Individual and Society

The contrast between Achilles and Hektor that weaves its way throughout the *Iliad* is really Homer's means of developing the conflict between individual values versus societal values. Achilles embodies the individual, alienated from his society, operating within the framework of his own code of pride and honor. He tends to represent passion and emotion. Like so many great epic heroes, he is ultimately not understandable. In contrast, Hektor, the great Trojan hero, is more human. He tends to exemplify reason over passion. He has a wife and son. He fights to save his city even though he knows the basis for the quarrel (Paris/Helen) is not worthy of the resulting destruction. Even in war, Hektor demonstrates more human qualities than Achilles. He hesitates; he gives ground; he is wounded; in the moment of crisis, he runs.

Readers see more of themselves in Hektor, the family man who cares about his commitments. Achilles, the estranged loner, lies outside the reader's comprehension.

Homer develops his comparison between the value systems of these two warriors. However, no simple explanation is possible. Achilles defeats Hektor, but Hektor is more understandable, and, in most cases, more admirable. Neither one "wins" in the sense that the ideas embodied in his character predominate at the end of the poem. In fact, the ideals and values of both characters are criticized and extolled. If the contrasting values of the individual versus society produce meaning, it is that both are necessary for a fully functioning community.

In terms of values, Hektor clearly upholds the norms of society. Book VI is justly famous for its presentation of Hektor with those close to him—his mother, Hekuba; his wife, Andromache; and his son, Astyanax. In this book there exists a tenderness and intimacy of feeling that occurs nowhere else in the *Iliad*. Society depends on the bonds of love and family, and Hektor encompasses and fights for those bonds. Andromache seems to urge Hektor to leave the battle, but fleeing destroys the values of the society even more surely than fighting and losing does.

In contrast, Achilles has only Briseis, a prize of war. She is a slave/concubine, and while she evinces emotion toward Achilles and Patroklos, there is no real relationship between them. Achilles withdraws from battle because of Briseis, but only because he feels cheated of booty. Achilles is the individual, acting on the basis of a personal code, with little concern for how his actions may affect the greater community. Achilles follows his personal feelings without regard for the consequences on the community at large; Hektor sees his actions within the context of the overall community.

In terms of motive, Hektor is once again more understandable. Hektor is motivated by responsibility and obligation. He may want to remain in the city with Andromache and Astyanax, but he knows his obligation is on the battlefield. He impresses the same obligation on Paris. Hektor runs from Achilles, but a sense of obligation, spurred by Athena, makes him turn. Hektor, the societal hero, makes decisions based on reason, and, in fact, his reason and sense of duty can overcome the emotions of fear and panic.

Achilles, in contrast, withdraws from battle over a slight. He returns for revenge. His motivations seem to be superficial, based on booty and more deeply on idiosyncrasy. The individual hero fights for his own reasons that others may not understand. When Achilles determines to fight, the outcome for himself and for others is secondary to his goal. Achilles even argues against eating before the battle, so single-minded is he after the death of Patroklos. Hektor's steadfastness in the face of fear is admirable; but overall, the maniacal manner of Achilles is more impressive and effective.

Finally, Hektor is more human. He questions himself in battle. He is not invincible, as his battle with Aias shows. He longs for peace, and he desperately fears the towering rage of Achilles. In simple terms he is a human hero with human faults. Achilles, in many ways, lacks ordinary human feelings. He remains on the sidelines when his friends beg him to return. In battle he is superhuman with no care for his own safety. He fears ignominious death from the River God but not death. Achilles' only human feelings are revealed when he returns Hektor's body to Priam.

In the end, this contrast between Hektor and Achilles shows the contrast between the values of the individual and the values of society. By the end of the Trojan War, both Hektor and Achilles are dead. Neither warrior by himself embodies the values that result in ultimate success. Perhaps those values inhere that most crafty warrior, Odysseus, who has a more perfect blending of individual skill and human emotion. In the *Iliad*, we may say that Hektor would make a better neighbor but Achilles a better soldier. Homer shows the need for both.

CliffsNotes Review

Use this CliffsNotes Review to test your understanding of the original text, and reinforce what you've learned in this book. After you work through the review and essay questions, identify the quote section, and the fun and useful practice projects, you're well on your way to understanding a comprehensive and meaningful interpretation of the *Iliad*.

Q&A

1. The theme announced at the start of the *Iliad* is

   a. sorrow

   b. war

   c. anger

   d. reconciliation

2. The Achaian warrior most noted for his skill in speech and tactics is:

   a. Odysseus

   b. Diomedes

   c. Telamonian Aias

   d. Idomeneus

3. What mistake does Patroklos make in his battle against the Trojans?

   a. He challenges Hektor

   b. He throws off his armor

   c. He curses Zeus

   d. He tries to storm the walls of Troy

4. Who pretends to be Hektor's brother, Deiphobus, and encourages him to fight Achilles?

a. Athena

b. Zeus

c. Aphrodite

d. Poseidon

5. On what day after the return of Hektor's body to the Trojans will the battle begin again?

a. tenth

b. eleventh

c. twelfth

d. fifteenth

Answers: 1. C 2. A 3. D 4. A 5. C

Fill in the Blanks

1. _____ is the wife of King Menelaos of Sparta; her abduction by Paris started the Trojan War.

2. A warrior's greatest day of battle is known as his _____.

3. Hektor's son is _____; his wife, _____.

4. The Trojan spy killed by Odysseus and Diomedes is _____.

5. The first Myrmidon to re-enter the battle is Achilles' companion, _____.

6. The new shield for Achilles is made by _____.

7. Hektor and Achilles fight before the _____ _____ at Troy.

8. Achilles finally returns Hektor's body to _____

Answers: 1. Helen 2. aristeia 3. Astyanax, Andromache 4. Dolon 5. Patroklos 6. Hephaistos 7. Scaean Gate 8. Priam

Identify the Quote

Identify each of the following quotations by explaining who the speaker is, what the situation is, and what the significance of the quote is. See answers at the end of the section.

1. "Rage—Goddess, sing the rage of Peleus' son Achilles."

2. "But I would die of shame to face the men of Troy and the Trojan women trailing their long robes if I would shrink from battle now, a coward. For in my heart and soul I also know this well: The day will come when sacred Troy must die, Priam must die, and all his people with him."

3. "Bring fire! Up with the war cries all together! Now Zeus hands *us* a day worth all the rest, today we seize these ships."

4. "So the immortals spun our lives that we, we wretched men live on to bear such torments—the gods live free of sorrows."

Answers: (1) [This quote opens the *Iliad*. Here the narrator calls on the Muse (Goddess) to literally sing through him the story of Achilles and his anger.]

(2) [Hektor is the speaker; he is talking to his wife, Andromache. He reveals his reasons for fighting and his fatalistic view of the war and answers her concerns about his returning to battle. Later he will add that no man has ever escaped fate. (Book VI)]

(3) [The speaker is Hektor. He is about to fire the Achaian ships. This marks the high point of Trojan success in the *Iliad*. (Book XV)]

(4) [The speaker is Achilles. He is speaking to Priam and relents in his anger against Hektor. He shows his understanding that all mortals suffer and feel sorrow in contrast to the gods. (Book XXIV)]

Essay Questions

1. Explain the quarrel between Agamemnon and Achilles in Book I.

2. What is the purpose of the catalogue of ships?

3. How does Book VI differ from most of the *Iliad*?

4. What is the purpose of the story of Diomedes, Odysseus, and Dolon in the overall plot of the *Iliad*?

5. Describe the shield of Achilles and explain the symbolism.

6. What is the significance of the speech of Achilles' horse?

7. What is a *theomachy*? Why does the theomachy occur?

8. Explain the clash of values symbolized in the fight between Achilles and Hektor.

9. How does Achilles change over the course of the poem?

Practice Projects

High School

1. Prepare a drawing or three-dimensional representation of the shield of Achilles. Include an explanation of the symbolism.

2. Do a research report with illustrations of Greek weapons and armor of the Mycenaean period.

College

1. Prepare a map showing the journey home of each of the Greek warriors who survive the Trojan war. Include an explanation of what eventually happens to each warrior.

2. Prepare a computer presentation on the evidence for and against the historical likelihood of the Trojan War.

CliffsNotes Resource Center

The learning doesn't need to stop here. CliffsNotes Resource Center shows you the best of the best—links to the best information in print and online about the author and/or related works. And don't think that this is all we've prepared for you; we've put all kinds of pertinent information at www.cliffsnotes.com. Look for all the terrific resources at your favorite bookstore or local library and on the Internet. When you're online, make your first stop www.cliffsnotes.com where you'll find more incredibly useful information about the *Iliad*.

Critical Works About Homer and the Epic

HOMER. The *Iliad*. Translated by Robert Fagles. Introduction and Notes by Bernard Knox. New York: Penguin Books, 1991.

BEYE, CHARLES ROWAN. *The Iliad, The Odyssey, and the Epic Tradition*. Garden City, N.Y., 1966. A highly recommended source for studying the epic tradition, particularly as it relates to Homer's works.

BOWRA, SIR MAURICE. *Tradition and Design in the Iliad*. Oxford, England, 1930. A useful source for understanding the epic convention. Bowra also looks at the characters from a different view than some other critics. He sees the fall of Troy as a result of Paris' violation of the social laws of marriage and the guest-host code.

JAYNES, JULIAN. *The Origin of Consciousness in the Breakdown of the Bicameral Mind*. Boston: Houghton Mifflin Company, 1990. A book about the development of consciouness in human beings. Jaynes has a long section on the *Iliad* in which he argues that the warriors are not truly conscious human beings and that their actions are directed by the gods who represent one side of the early, bicameral human mind. A really different view of the poem.

REDFIELD, JAMES M. *Nature and Culture in the "Iliad": The Tragedy of Hector*. Chicago: University of Chicago Press, 1975. A good source for early cultural practices and the purposes of rituals and ceremony. Generally quite readable, but some of the concepts may take re-reading for the less experienced reader.

STEINER, GEORGE, and ROBERT FAGLES (eds.). *Homer: A Collection of Critical Essays.* Englewood Cliffs, NJ.: Collier Books, 1962.

WILLOCK, MALCOLM W. *A Companion to the "Iliad," Based on the Translation by Richard Lattimore.* Chicago: University of Chicago Press, 1976. Very helpful in identifying obscure names of places, people, and gods. Some explanation of the epic's organization, as well as an explanation of the purpose of some important incidents with background explanations.

WOOD, MICHAEL. *In Search of the Trojan War.* New York: Facts on File Publications, 1985. An interesting survey of archaeological findings on the historic city of Troy. The book contains much information on the *Iliad*, the myths, and the archaeology. It was made into a mini-series by the BBC.

WRIGHT, JOHN, ed. *Essays on the "Iliad."* Bloomington, Indiana: Indiana University Press, 1978. Several good essays in this collection. The last five are particularly useful for understanding the gods and Homer's themes.

Internet

Check out these Web resources for more information about Homer and the *Iliad*.

Encyclopedia Mythica, `http://pantheon.org/mythica/areas/greek/` —has a searchable index of Greek mythological characters and a link to Greek legendary heroes. Also includes genealogical charts for both gods and hero's, including Achilles, Priam, and Helen. Six hundred Greek myth articles and 446 heroic legend articles. Great site to find quick information on names.

Perseus Project, `http://www.perseus.tufts.edu/` — a huge Web site for all things ancient—a beginning portal for information on the cultural, historical, and artistic background of most ancient societies. This is one of the premiere sites on the Internet.

The Virtual Iliad, `http://hyperion.advanced.org/19300/data/iliad.htm` —provides a long prose synopsis of the *Iliad* with interior links to explanations, pictures, and pronunciations. Essays on Homeric warfare, the role of the Gods, and similes and metaphors are also included. Links to *The Virtual Odyssey*.

The Homeric Epics Page, `http://sites.netscape.net/ bethanthomas/homer` —This site has a good presentation on themes related to the gods in the *Iliad*; is still under construction.

The Classics Page, `http://www.users.globalnet.co.uk/~loxias/ iliad/iliadstart3.htm` —contains good review material on several classic works including, the *Iliad*. Of special interest is an interactive review/game on the *Iliad*.

Part of **The Prehistoric Archaeology of the Aegean** *Web site at Dartmouth*, `http://devlab.dartmouth.edu/history/bronze_age/ lessons/27.html` —presents a detailed discussion of the archaeological discoveries at Troy site VIIA. Good information on the historicity of the Trojan War.

The Online Medieval and Classical Library—Hesiod, the Homeric Hymns and Homerica; The Cypria, `http://sunsite. berkeley.edu/OMACL/Hesiod/cypria.html` — the text of the *Cypria*, which contains much information on the story of the Trojan War that is not included in the *Iliad*. The *Cypria* is the source for the story that the Achaians made two different attempts on Troy about eight years apart.

Videos

The Iliad and the Trojan War, (Educational Video Network).

In Search of the Trojan War, Michael Wood.

Send Us Your Favorite Tips

In your quest for knowledge, have you ever experienced that sublime moment when you figure out a trick that saves time or trouble? Perhaps you realized you were taking ten steps to accomplish something that could have taken two. Or you found a little-known workaround that achieved great results. If you've discovered a useful tip that helped you appreciate Homer's *Iliad* more effectively and you'd like to share it, the CliffsNotes staff would love to hear from you. Go to our Web site at www.cliffsnotes.com and click the Talk to Us button. If we select your tip, we may publish it as part of CliffsNotes Daily, our exciting, free e-mail newsletter. To find out more or to subscribe to a newsletter, go to www.cliffsnotes.com on the Web.

Index

A

Achaians, 4

Achilles
Achaians, refuses to help, 52
Achaians, rejoins, 67
Agamemnon, quarrel with, 23, 48, 49, 84
Agamemnon, reconciliation with, 47, 68, 103
alienation, 102, 105
aristeia, 71
armor, 10, 60, 62, 64, 94
Briseis, 22, 67, 105
capacity for feeling, 65, 106
death, 67, 69, 104
fate, warned of, 8
heel, 9
Hektor, contrasted with, 76, 101, 104, 105, 106
Hektor, duels with, 75, 94
Hektor foil to, 92
Hektor, kills, 75
Hektor, mutilates corpse of, 75, 81, 85, 86
Hera saves from drowning, 73
hero/anti-hero, 58, 67
honor, 61, 99
horses, 61, 62, 67, 69
introduced, 14
killed, 10
kinship, recognition of, 104
Lykaon, kills, 72
Meursault (The Stranger) compared, 104
motivations, 106
Odysseus foil to, 89
opposites, embodiment of, 102
Patroklos' death, effect on, 85
Patroklos' death, responsibility for, 49
Patroklos' ghost visits, 79
Patroklos alter ego to, 102
Patroklos, avenges, 64, 65
Patroklos, relationship with, 86, 87
Priam, reconciliation with, 81, 82, 96
pride, 48, 52, 85
quotes, 109
revenge, 48
river battle, 72, 85
sense of responsibility, 100
sense of social order, 84
wine cup, 61
wrath, as childish, 52
wrath, as irrational fury, 79
wrath, as principal theme, 22, 23, 101
wrath, ends, 81, 82, 103
wrath, first, 65
wrath, initiated by honor, 101
wrath, reaches height, 85
wrath, second, 65

Aeneas, 11, 16, 36, 70

Aeneid (Virgil), 3, 38, 70

Agamemnon
Achilles, quarrel with, 23, 48, 49, 84
Achilles, reconciliation with, 47, 68, 103
adequacy as leader, 28
aristeia, 53
Artemis, offends, 9
Briseis, 23
demoralization, 47
dream, 27, 28
family order, importance of, 88
Hamlet compared, 49
historical existence, 4
introduced, 15
Iphigeneia sacrifice, 9
madness, 49
Menelaos, bond with, 39
Odysseus foil to, 89
Priam, sacrifices with, 30
role as king, 88, 89
sense of responsibility, 100
weakness, 88
wounded, 52, 55
Zeus, contrasted with, 58

Agenor, 72, 73

Aias (Ajax), 10, 15, 43

Aias the Lesser, 15

aidos (fear of disgrace), 100

Alexandros, 7

ambrosia , 18

Andromache, 16, 39, 92

Antenor, 17, 43

Antigone (Sophocles), 49, 53

Antilochos, 15

Aphrodite
Athena, defeated by, 72
Diomedes wounds, 36
Hektor's body, protects, 78
Helen's carnality, symbol of, 31
Hera, sash given to, 57
introduced, 18
Paris, offers Helen to, 8
Trojans, aids, 36, 38

Apollo, 19, 22, 50, 51, 60, 78

Ares, 19, 36, 72

aristeia (greatest moment in battle), 14, 37

armor. *See also* weaponry descriptions
association with identity, 40
descriptions of, 66
exchange of, 39, 57, 94
victor claims, 45, 62

NOTES

CliffsNotes

LITERATURE NOTES

The Odyssey
Oedipus Trilogy
Of Human Bondage
Of Mice and Men
The Old Man and
the Sea
Old Testament
Oliver Twist
The Once and
Future King
One Day in the Life of
Ivan Denisovich
One Flew Over the
Cuckoo's Nest
100 Years of Solitude
O'Neill's Plays
Othello
Our Town
The Outsiders
The Ox Bow Incident
Paradise Lost
A Passage to India
The Pearl
The Pickwick Papers
The Picture of
Dorian Gray
Pilgrim's Progress
The Plague
Plato's Euthyphro…
Plato's The Republic
Poe's Short Stories
A Portrait of the
Artist…
The Portrait of a Lady
The Power and
the Glory
Pride and Prejudice
The Prince
The Prince and
the Pauper
A Raisin in the Sun
The Red Badge of
Courage
The Red Pony
The Return of the
Native
Richard II
Richard III

The Rise of
Silas Lapham
Robinson Crusoe
Roman Classics
Romeo and Juliet
The Scarlet Letter
A Separate Peace
Shakespeare's
Comedies
Shakespeare's Histories
Shakespeare's
Minor Plays
Shakespeare's Sonnets
Shakespeare's Tragedies
Shaw's Pygmalion &
Arms…
Silas Marner
Sir Gawain…Green
Knight
Sister Carrie
Slaughterhouse-Five
Snow Falling on Cedars
Song of Solomon
Sons and Lovers
The Sound and the Fury
Steppenwolf &
Siddhartha
The Stranger
The Sun Also Rises
T.S. Eliot's Poems &
Plays
A Tale of Two Cities
The Taming of the
Shrew
Tartuffe, Misanthrope…
The Tempest
Tender Is the Night
Tess of the D'Urbervilles
Their Eyes Were
Watching God
Things Fall Apart
The Three Musketeers
To Kill a Mockingbird
Tom Jones
Tom Sawyer
Treasure Island &
Kidnapped
The Trial

Tristram Shandy
Troilus and Cressida
Twelfth Night
Ulysses
Uncle Tom's Cabin
The Unvanquished
Utopia
Vanity Fair
Vonnegut's Works
Waiting for Godot
Walden
Walden Two
War and Peace
Who's Afraid of
Virginia…
Winesburg, Ohio
The Winter's Tale
The Woman Warrior
Worldly Philosophers
Wuthering Heights
A Yellow Raft in
Blue Water

Check Out the All-New CliffsNotes Guides

TECHNOLOGY TOPICS

Balancing Your Check-
book with Quicken
Buying and Selling
on eBay
Buying Your First PC
Creating a Winning
PowerPoint 2000
Presentation
Creating Web Pages
with HTML
Creating Your First
Web Page
Exploring the World
with Yahoo!
Getting on the Internet
Going Online with AOL
Making Windows 98
Work for You

Setting Up a
Windows 98
Home Network
Shopping Online Safely
Upgrading and
Repairing Your PC
Using Your First iMac
Using Your First PC
Writing Your First
Computer Program

PERSONAL FINANCE TOPICS

Budgeting & Saving
Your Money
Getting a Loan
Getting Out of Debt
Investing for the
First Time
Investing in
401(k) Plans
Investing in IRAs
Investing in
Mutual Funds
Investing in the
Stock Market
Managing Your Money
Planning Your
Retirement
Understanding
Health Insurance
Understanding
Life Insurance

CAREER TOPICS

Delivering a Winning
Job Interview
Finding a Job
on the Web
Getting a Job
Writing a Great Resume